MW00445375

21 crocheted
TANKS & TUNICS

0 11557 01483 9

21 crocheted TANKS & TUNICS

SANDI ROSNER

STACKPOLE
BOOKS

Copyright © 2016 by Sandra Rosner

Published by
STACKPOLE BOOKS
An imprint of Rowman & Littlefield
Distributed by National Book Network

All rights reserved, including the right to reproduce this book or portions thereof in any form or by any means, electronic or mechanical, including recording or by any information storage and retrieval system, without permission in writing from the publisher.

The contents of this book are for personal use only. Patterns contained herein may be reproduced in limited quantities for such use. Any large-scale commercial reproduction is prohibited without the written consent of the publisher.

Printed in the United States of America

10 9 8 7 6 5 4 3 2 1

First edition

Cover design: Caroline Stover
Model photography: Tom Moore
Stylist: Alison Wilkes
Hair and make-up: Rex Tucker Moss
Jewelry: Connie Verrusio, earrings shown in photos for Clement and Sansome, and necklaces shown in photos of Folsom and Marina.

Library of Congress Cataloging-in-Publication Data

Names: Rosner, Sandi, author.
Title: 21 crocheted tanks & tunics : stylish designs for every occasion / Sandi Rosner.
Other titles: Twenty one crocheted tanks and tunics
Description: First edition. | Mechanicsburg, PA : Stackpole Books, 2016. | Includes bibliographical references and index.
Identifiers: LCCN 2015041884 | ISBN 9780811714839 (pbk. : alk. paper)
Subjects: LCSH: Crocheting--Patterns. | Women's clothing.
Classification: LCC TT825 .R664 2016 | DDC 746.43/4--dc23 LC record available at http://lccn.loc.gov/2015041884

This book is dedicated to Olga Ramona Essex,
who taught me to value beautiful things made by hand.

Contents

Acknowledgments

I am fortunate to have many talented and generous people in my life who have contributed to the making of this book. Special thanks are due to:

- Pam Hoenig and her team at Stackpole Books, for editorial stewardship
- Rita Greenfeder, for her patient technical editing
- Tom Moore, for his beautiful photographs
- Amy Gunderson, who has been a conduit for many good things in my life
- Candi Jensen, who brought me back to crochet, sometimes against my will
- Diane Brown, for her steadfast friendship and support

Introduction

Whether you call them tank tops or camisoles, sleeveless tops have become wardrobe staples. Worn on its own, a tank can make sultry weather more comfortable. Layered over another top or under a jacket when the temperature dips, a camisole adds color and texture to a simple outfit. The sculptural nature of crochet makes it a wonderful medium for designing these versatile tops.

My personal style tends toward the classic and conservative, and you'll find pieces in this collection that fit that mold. I think of these as "grown-up" tops, with wider shoulders and high armholes that won't expose your underwear. You can easily toss them on over a skirt or pair of jeans and go.

If you tend to gravitate toward funkier, more contemporary silhouettes, this book contains pieces for you, too. With skinny straps, asymmetrical hemlines, and interesting wraps, these tanks would be right at home with shorts or a maxi skirt at a summer music festival.

Whatever your style or your skill level, I hope you'll find pieces in this collection that you want to make part of your wardrobe. My goal is not to design cool projects, but to design clothing you actually want to wear. It is my wish that you will enjoy working with this book and will end up with a closet full of tanks, tunics, and camisoles you are proud to say you made yourself.

Yarn

The yarns selected for the projects in this book are what I think of as "summer yarns"—cotton, linen, silk, rayon, and blends of those fibers. These yarns create cool, airy fabrics and make stitchwork pop.

Standard Yarn Weight System

Categories of yarn, gauge ranges, and recommended needle and hook sizes

Yarn Weight Symbol & Category Names	0 LACE	1 SUPER FINE	2 FINE	3 LIGHT	4 MEDIUM	5 BULKY	6 SUPER BULKY	7 JUMBO
Type of Yarns in Category	Fingering, 10-Count Crochet Thread	Sock, Fingering, Baby	Sport, Baby	DK, Light Worsted	Worsted, Afghan, Aran	Chunky, Craft, Rug	Bulky, Roving	Jumbo, Roving
Knit Gauge Range in Stockinette Stitch to 4 inches*	33–40 sts**	27–32 sts	23–26 sts	21–24 st	16–20 sts	12–15 sts	7–11 sts	6 sts and fewer
Recommended Needle in Metric Size Range	1.5–2.25 mm	2.25–3.25 mm	3.25–3.75 mm	3.75–4.5 mm	4.5–5.5 mm	5.5–8 mm	8–12.75 mm	12.75 mm and larger
Recommended Needle in U.S. Size Range	000 to 1	1 to 3	3 to 5	5 to 7	7 to 9	9 to 11	11 to 17	17 and larger
Crochet Gauge Ranges in Single Crochet to 4 inches*	32–42 double crochets**	21–32 sts	16–20 sts	12–17 sts	11–14 sts	8–11 sts	7–9 sts	6 sts and fewer
Recommended Hook in Metric Size Range	Steel*** 1.6–1.4 mm Regular hook 2.25 mm	2.25–3.5 mm	3.5–4.5 mm	4.5–5.5 mm	5.5–6.5 mm	6.5–9 mm	9–15 mm	15 mm and larger
Recommended Hook in U.S. Size Range	Steel 6, 7, 8*** Regular hook B–1	B–1 to E–4	E–4 to 7	7 to I–9	I–9 to K–10½	K–10½ to M–13	M–13 to Q	Q and larger

* GUIDELINES ONLY: The above reflect the most commonly used gauges and needle or hook sizes for specific yarn categories.

** Lace weight yarns are usually knitted or crocheted on larger needles and hooks to create lacy, openwork patterns. Accordingly, a gauge range is difficult to determine. Always follow the gauge stated in your pattern.

*** Steel crochet hooks are sized differently from regular hooks—the higher the number, the smaller the hook, which is the reverse of regular hook sizing.

Source: Craft Yarn Council of America's www.YarnStandards.com

Of course, you should feel free to use whatever yarn you wish for your crochet projects. When making substitutions, consider fiber content and yarn construction as well as gauge. When we crochet or knit, we are creating a fabric with unique qualities of texture and drape. A polyester chenille may work to the same gauge as a plied linen, but you'll have a very different fabric. These differences will affect the way the finished piece fits and hangs on the body. When in doubt, make a generous swatch with the yarn in the stitch pattern you are considering. Evaluate the swatch critically. Ask yourself if you'll be happy wearing a tank or camisole made with this fabric.

Many of the yarns I've used are machine washable, which is a great attribute for any garment worn in warm weather. But beware: Yarns made with lots of cotton and/or linen may shrink when laundered. If you don't take this shrinkage into account, you'll be disappointed when your tank fits only until you first wash it.

For the samples made with machine washable yarns, I "blocked" both my gauge swatches and my finished samples by adding them to a regular load of laundry and running them through the washer and dryer. I wanted to be sure I was treating them just as I would if they were part of my wardrobe. This laundering caused most of the cotton and linen pieces to shrink, some significantly so.

The gauge shown in the patterns for all the designs is "after blocking." That means that the gauge includes shrinkage in the wash. While you are making the piece, it will look too big and too long. Don't worry–if your "after blocking" gauge matches the gauge specified in the pattern, your piece will shrink to the correct size when you wash it.

Of course, the care you give the finished garment should be governed by the care instructions on the yarn label. While most of the cotton and linen yarns will happily tolerate machine washing and drying, some projects are made with more delicate fibers that will require hand washing. When in doubt, refer to the label on your yarn.

Gauge

Gauge is listed for each design in this book. This is simply a statement of how many stitches and how many rows are needed to make a 4"/10 cm square using the yarn and stitch pattern specified. If you do not match this gauge your tank will not turn out the size you planned. Isn't it worth a small investment of time up front to make sure your time isn't wasted making a piece that doesn't fit?

The yarn amounts called for in these patterns include a bit extra for use in testing your gauge.

To test your gauge, begin by making a swatch at least 5"/12.7 cm square in the pattern stitch indicated. Block your swatch by washing and drying it the way you intend to wash and dry the finished garment. Then measure off a 4"/10 cm square in the center of your swatch and count the stitches and rows. If you have more stitches in 4"/10 cm than the pattern specifies, use a larger hook. If you have fewer stitches in 4"/10 cm than is called for, use a smaller hook. Adjust your hook size until you can match the gauge specification.

Fit

The bust measurement listed for each pattern is the actual finished garment measurement.

These tanks and tunics are intended to comfortably skim the body, with a fit that is neither skin tight nor oversized. To achieve this fit, choose the size which is closest to, but not smaller than, your actual bust measurement. If you are making one of the longer tunic designs, base your size choice on the larger of your bust or hip measurement.

Abbreviations

ch	chain
dc	double crochet
dc2tog	double crochet 2 together
dec	decrease (d)
hdc	half double crochet
hdc2tog	half double crochet 2 together
hdc3tog	half double crochet 3 together
inc	increase (d)
patt	pattern
rem	remain (s) (ing)
rep	repeat
rnd(s)	round(s)
RS	right side
sc	single crochet
sc2tog	single crochet 2 together
sc3tog	single crochet 3 together
sk	skip
sl st	slip stitch
sp(s)	space(s)
st(s)	stitch(es)
WS	wrong side
yo	yarn over

Projects

Folsom

I s there any silhouette more flattering than a wrap? With its deep V-neck and built-in waist definition, this feminine top will pair well with tailored skirts and pants.

SKILL LEVEL
Intermediate

SIZES
Women's Extra Small (Small, Medium, Large, Extra Large, 2X Large)

FINISHED MEASUREMENTS
Bust: 32 (36$\frac{1}{2}$, 40, 44$\frac{1}{2}$, 48, 52$\frac{1}{2}$)"/81.5 (93, 101.5, 113, 122, 133.5) cm

YARN
Patons Silk Bamboo, light weight #3 yarn (70% viscose from bamboo, 30% silk; 102 yd./2.2 oz., 93 m/65 g per skein)
- 6 (7, 8, 9, 10, 11) skeins #85219 Sea

HOOKS & NOTIONS
- US size H-8/5 mm crochet hook
- Removable stitch markers or safety pins
- Tapestry needle

GAUGE
14 sts and 11 rows in Brick Stitch patt = 4"/10 cm

PATTERN NOTES
- Folsom is worked in one piece from the bottom up. The only seams are at the shoulders.
- The stitch count in this pattern changes from row to row. Count stitches at the end of RS double crochet rows only.
- Turning chain is not counted as a stitch.

STITCH PATTERN

Brick Stitch Pattern
Row 1 (WS): Ch1, sc in first dc, ch2, sk next dc, sc in sp between last skipped st and next dc, *ch2, sk next 2 dc, sc in sp between last skipped st and next dc; rep from * to end, ending with sc in 3rd ch of beginning ch-3.
Row 2 (RS): Ch3, 2 dc in each ch-2 sp to last ch-2 sp, dc in last ch-2 sp, dc in last sc.
Rep Rows 1–2 for patt.

Back

Ch 169 (189, 211, 231, 253, 273).

Row 1 (RS): Dc in 4th ch from hook, dc in each ch to end.
166 (186, 208, 228, 250, 270) dc.

Work 5 rows in Brick St patt.

Next row (RS): Ch3, [2 dc in ch-2 sp] 26 times, place marker,
[2 dc in ch-2 sp] 31 times, place marker, 2 dc in each ch-2
sp to end.

Next row (WS): Work Row 1 of Brick St patt.

Next row (Dec row): *Work in patt to ch-2 sp before marker,
1 dc in next 2 ch-2 sps, moving marker to between these
2 dc; rep from * once, work in patt to end. 4 sts dec.

Continuing in patt, rep Dec row every RS row 7 more
times. 134 (154, 176, 196, 218, 238) dc.

Work Row 1 of Brick St patt.

Shape Front Wrap

Row 1 (RS): Ch3, dc2tog in first 2 ch-2 sps, *work in patt to
ch-2 sp before marker, dc3 in next ch-2 sp twice, moving
marker to between these two 3-dc groups; rep from *
once, work in patt to last 2 ch-2 sps, dc2tog in last 2
ch-2 sps.

Row 2 (WS): Work Row 1 of Brick St patt.

Row 3: Ch3, dc2tog in first 2 ch-2 sps, work in patt to last 2
ch-2 sps, dc2tog in last 2 ch-2 sps. 4 sts dec.

Row 4: Rep Row 2.

Rep [Rows 1–4] 4 more times. 114 (134, 156, 176, 198, 218)
dc.

Shape Right Front Neck
and Armhole

Row 1 (RS): Ch3, dc2tog in first 2 ch-2 sps, [2 dc in ch-2 sp]
11 (13, 17, 20, 23, 26) times, dc2tog in next 2 ch-2 sps,
turn. 26 (30, 38, 44, 50, 56) dc.

Row 2: Work Row 1 of Brick St patt.

Rep [Rows 1–2] 1 (2, 3, 4, 5, 6) more times. 18 (18, 22, 24, 26,
28) dc.

Next row (RS): Ch3, dc2tog in first 2 ch-2 sps, work in patt to
end.

Next row: Work Row 1 of Brick St patt.

Rep last 2 rows 5 (7, 7, 8, 9) more times. 6 (6, 6, 8, 8, 8) dc.

Work 4 (2, 0, 0, 0, 0) rows even in Brick St patt.

Fasten off.

Shape Left Front Neck and Armhole

With RS facing, sk 3 (4, 5, 5, 6, 7) ch-2 sps for armhole and rejoin yarn.

Row 1 (RS): Ch3, dc2tog in first 2 ch-2 sps, 2 dc in each ch-2 sp to last 2 ch-2 sps, dc2tog in next 2 ch-2 sps, turn. 26 (30, 38, 44, 50, 56) dc.

Row 2: Work Row 1 of Brick St patt.

Rep [Rows 1–2] 1 (2, 3, 4, 5, 6) more times. 18 (18, 22, 24, 26, 28) dc.

Next row (RS): Ch3, 2 dc in each ch-2 sp to last 2 ch-2 sps, dc2tog in next 2 ch-2 sps.

Next row: Work Row 1 of Brick St patt.

Rep last 2 rows 5 (5, 7, 7, 8, 9) more times. 6 (6, 6, 8, 8, 8) dc.

Work 4 (2, 0, 0, 0, 0) rows even in patt.

Fasten off.

Finishing

Sew shoulder seams.

Ties

Join yarn at beginning of right front wrap shaping. Ch 40 (45, 50, 55, 60, 65). Fasten off.

Join yarn at beginning of left front wrap shaping. Ch 110 (120, 130, 140, 150, 160). Fasten off.

Front and Neck Edging

Join yarn at lower right front corner. Sc evenly along front edge to tie, sc in each st of ch, sc3 in end of ch, sc along other side of ch, sc around neck edge to tie at left front, sc in each st of ch, sc3 in end of ch, sc along other side of ch, sc down left front to lower edge. Fasten off.

Armhole Edging

Join yarn at center of underarm and work 1 rnd of sc around armhole edge. Fasten off.

Weave in ends. Block.

Back

With RS facing, sk 3 (4, 5, 5, 6, 7) ch-2 sps for armhole and rejoin yarn.

Row 1 (RS): Ch3, dc2tog in first 2 ch-2 sps, [2 dc in ch-2 sp] 21 (24, 26, 30, 32, 35) times, dc2tog in next 2 ch-2 sps, turn. 46 (52, 56, 64, 68, 74) dc.

Row 2 (WS): Work Row 1 of Brick St patt.

Rep [Rows 1–2] 1 (2, 3, 4, 5, 6) more times. 42 (44, 44, 48, 48, 50) dc.

Work even until same length as right front to shoulder, ending with a WS row.

Fasten off.

Valencia

ere is a classic that belongs in every wardrobe. The scoop neck, waist shaping, and scalloped edging elevate this tank beyond the basic. You'll want to live in it all summer long.

SKILL LEVEL
Easy

SIZES
Women's Extra Small (Small, Medium, Large, Extra Large, 2X Large)

FINISHED MEASUREMENTS
Bust: 29^1/$_4$ (33^1/$_2$, 37^3/$_4$, 42^1/$_4$, 46^1/$_2$, 50^3/$_4$)"/74.5 (85.5, 96, 107, 118, 128.5) cm

YARN
Universal Yarn Cotton Supreme DK, light weight #3 yarn (100% cotton; 230 yd./3.5 oz., 210 m/100 g per skein)
- 2 (3, 3, 4, 4, 4) skeins #702 Ecru

HOOKS & NOTIONS
- US size H-8/5 mm crochet hook
- Tapestry needle

GAUGE
15 sts and 11 rows in hdc = 4"/10 cm

PATTERN NOTES
- Turning chain is not included in stitch counts.
- See pages 87 and 88 for photo tutorial on hdc and hdc2tog.

Back

Ch 59 (67, 75, 83, 91, 99).
Row 1 (RS): Hdc in 3rd ch from hook and in each ch to end. 57 (65, 73, 81, 89, 97) hdc.
Row 2: Ch2 (does not count as a st), hdc in each st to end.
Rep Row 2 for patt.
Work even until piece measures 2"/5 cm, ending with a WS row.

Shape Waist

Next row (Dec row) (RS): Ch2, hdc2tog over first 2 sts, hdc to last 2 sts, hdc2tog. 2 sts dec.
Rep Dec row every RS row 3 more times. 49 (57, 65, 73, 81, 89) sts.

Work even until piece measures 7"/18 cm, ending with a
  WS row.
Next row (Inc row) (RS): Ch2, 2 hdc in first st, hdc to last st,
  2 hdc in last st. 2 sts inc.
Rep Inc row every RS row 3 more times. 57 (65, 73, 81, 89,
  97) sts.
Work even until piece measures 13"/33 cm, ending with a
  WS row, and ending last row 3 (4, 5, 6, 7, 8) sts before end.

Shape Armholes

Row 1 (RS): Ch2, hdc in each st to last 3 (4, 5, 6, 7, 8) sts.
Row 2 (Dec row) (WS): Ch2, hdc2tog over first 2 sts, hdc to
  last 2 sts, hdc2tog. 2 sts dec.
Rep Dec row every row 3 (5, 7, 9, 11, 13) more times. 43
  (45, 47, 49, 51, 53) sts.
Work even until armholes measure 4 (4$^1/_2$, 5, 5$^1/_2$, 6,
  6$^1/_2$)"/10 (11.5, 12.5, 14, 15, 16.5) cm, ending with a WS
  row.

Shape Back Neck

Row 1 (RS): Ch2, hdc in next 10 (11, 11, 12, 13, 14) sts,
  hdc2tog over next 2 sts. Continue on these 11 (12, 12,
  13, 14, 15) sts only for right back shoulder.
Row 2 (WS): Ch2, hdc2tog over first 2 sts, hdc to end.
Row 3: Ch2, hdc in each st to last 2 sts, hdc2tog.
Row 4: Ch2, hdc2tog over first 2 sts, hdc to end. 8 (9, 9, 10,
  11, 12) sts.
Row 5: Ch2, hdc to end. Fasten off.

Left Back Shoulder

Sk 19 (19, 21, 21, 21, 21) sts at center neck and rejoin yarn
  for left back shoulder.
Row 1 (RS): Ch2, hdc2tog over first 2 sts, hdc to end. 11 (12,
  12, 13, 14, 15) sts.
Row 2 (WS): Ch2, hdc in each st to last 2 sts, hdc2tog.
Row 3: Ch2, hdc2tog over first 2 sts, hdc to end.
Row 4: Ch2, hdc in each st to last 2 sts, hdc2tog. 8 (9, 9, 10,
  11, 12) sts.
Row 5: Ch2, hdc to end. Fasten off.

Row 2 (WS): Ch2, hdc2tog over first 2 sts, work in patt to end. 1 st dec at neck edge.

Rep these 2 rows 2 more times. 6 sts dec at neck edge total.

When armhole and neck shaping is complete, 8 (9, 9, 10, 11, 12) sts remain.

Work even until same length as back. Fasten off.

Right Front Shoulder

Sk 15 (15, 17, 17, 17, 17) marked sts at center neck and rejoin yarn for right front shoulder.

Row 1 (RS): Ch2, hdc2tog over first 2 sts, work in patt to end, continuing armhole shaping if necessary. 1 st dec at neck edge.

Row 2 (WS): Work in patt to last 2 sts, hdc2tog. 1 st dec at neck edge.

Rep these 2 rows 2 more times. 6 sts dec at neck edge total.

When armhole and neck shaping is complete, 8 (9, 9, 10, 11, 12) sts remain.

Work even until same length as back. Fasten off.

Finishing

Sew side seams. Sew shoulder seams.

Neck Edging

Join yarn at right shoulder seam. Work 1 rnd sc around neck edge. Count sts and adjust if necessary to make the total a multiple of 4 sts.

Next rnd: *Sk 1, 5 hdc in next st, sk 1, sl st in next st; rep from * to end of rnd. Fasten off.

Armhole Edging

Join yarn at side seam. Work 1 rnd sc around armhole edge. Count sts and adjust if necessary to make the total a multiple of 4 sts.

Next rnd: *Sk 1, 5 hdc in next st, sk 1, sl st in next st; rep from * to end of rnd.

Fasten off.

Hem Edging

Join yarn at side seam. Work 1 rnd sc around hem edge. Count sts and adjust if necessary to make the total a multiple of 4 sts.

Next rnd: *Sk 1, 5 hdc in next st, sk 1, sl st in next st; rep from * to end of rnd.

Fasten off.

Weave in ends. Block lightly.

Front

Work same as for Back until armhole measures 2 (2^1/$_2$, 3, 3, 3^1/$_2$, 3^1/$_2$)"/5 (6.5, 7.5, 7.5, 9, 9) cm, ending with a WS row.

NOTE: For sizes Medium, Large, Extra Large, and 2X Large, front neck shaping begins before armhole shaping is complete.

Shape Front Neck

Mark center 15 (15, 17, 17, 17, 17) sts. Continue armhole shaping if necessary while working neck shaping.

Row 1 (RS): Work in patt to 2 sts before marked sts, hdc2tog. 1 st dec at neck edge. Continue on these sts only for left front shoulder.

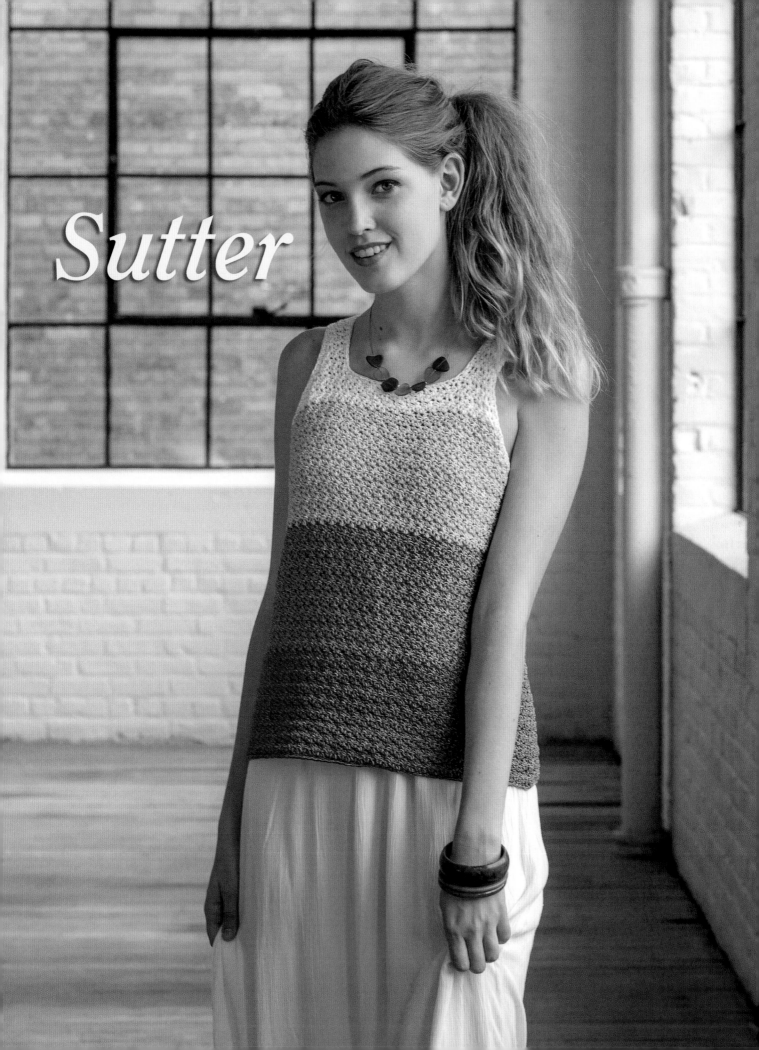

Sutter

This is an elegant top that is all about the yarn. The simple shape comes alive with gradient color and subtle sparkle.

SKILL LEVEL
Easy

SIZES
Women's Extra Small (Small, Medium, Large, Extra Large)

FINISHED MEASUREMENTS
Bust: 31^1/$_2$ (36, 39^1/$_2$, 44, 47^1/$_2$)"/80 (91.5, 100, 112, 120.5) cm

YARN
Berroco Captiva Metallic, medium weight #4 yarn (45% cotton, 23% polyester, 19% acrylic, 12% rayon, 1% other; 98 yd./1.75 oz., 90 m/50 g per skein)
- 2 (2, 3, 3, 3) skeins #7542 Antique Copper (A)
- 2 (2, 3, 3, 3) skeins #7540 Mascarpone (C)

Berroco Captiva, medium weight #4 yarn (60% cotton, 23% polyester, 17% acrylic; 98 yd./1.75 oz., 90 m/50 g per skein)
- 2 (2, 2, 3, 3) skeins #5506 Bronze (B)
- 1 (1, 1, 2, 2) skeins #5501 Venetian Lace (D)

HOOKS & NOTIONS
- US size I-9/5.5 mm crochet hook
- Tapestry needle

GAUGE
14 sts and 13 rows in Hi-Lo patt = 4"/10 cm

PATTERN NOTE
- Turning chain is not included in stitch counts.

STITCH PATTERN

Hi-Lo Pattern
Row 1: Ch1, *sc in dc, dc in sc; rep from * to end.
Rep Row 1 for patt.

Back

With A, ch 57 (65, 71, 79, 85).

Set-up row (WS): Sc in 2nd ch from hook and in each ch to end. 56 (64, 70, 78, 84) sts.

Begin working Hi-Lo patt.

When piece measures 5 (5, 5^1/$_2$, 5^1/$_2$, 6)"/12.5 (12.5, 14, 14, 15) cm, change to B.

Continue in Hi-Lo patt.

When piece measures 10 (10, 11, 11, 12)"/25.5 (25.5, 28, 28, 30.5) cm, change to C.

Continue in Hi-Lo patt until piece measures 13^1/$_2$ (13, 14^1/$_2$, 14, 15^1/$_2$)"/34.5 (33, 37, 35.5, 39.5) cm, ending with a WS row and ending last row 3 (4, 5, 6, 6) sts before end.

Shape Armholes

NOTE: The color is changed before armhole shaping is complete. Please read ahead.

Row 1 (RS): Ch1, work in established Hi-Lo patt to last 3 (4, 5, 6, 6) sts, turn work.

Rows 2–3: Ch 1, work in established Hi-Lo patt to last 2 (2, 2, 3, 4) sts, turn work. 46 (52, 56, 60, 64) sts.

Row 4 (Dec row): Ch1, sc2tog, *sc in dc, dc in sc; rep from * to last 3 sts, sc2tog, dc. 2 sts dec.

Rep Dec row every row 6 (8, 9, 10, 11) more times. 32 (34, 36, 38, 40) sts.

AT THE SAME TIME, when piece measures 15 (15, 16^1/$_2$, 16^1/$_2$, 18)"/38 (38, 42, 42, 45.5) cm, change to D.

Work even in patt until armhole measures 4^1/$_2$ (5, 5^1/$_2$, 6, 6^1/$_2$)"/11.5 (12.5, 14, 15, 16.5) cm, ending with a WS row.

Shape Back Neck

Next row (RS): Work 6 sts in patt, turn work. Continue on these sts only for right back shoulder.

Work 7 more rows even in patt. Fasten off.

Sk 20 (22, 24, 26, 28) sts at center neck and rejoin yarn for left back shoulder.

Work over remaining 6 sts only.

Work 8 rows even in patt. Fasten off.

Front

Work same as for back until armhole measures 3 (3^1/$_2$, 4, 4^1/$_2$, 5)"/7.5 (9, 10, 11.5, 12.5) cm, ending with a WS row.

NOTE: For all sizes except Extra Large, front neck shaping begins before armhole shaping is complete. Please read ahead.

Shape Front Neck

Mark center 20 (22, 24, 26, 28) sts.

Next row (RS): Work in patt to marked sts, turn work. Continue on these sts only for left front shoulder.

Continuing armhole shaping if necessary, work in patt until same length as back to shoulder. When all armhole shaping is complete, 6 sts remain. Fasten off.

Sk 20 (22, 24, 26, 28) marked sts at center neck and rejoin yarn for right front shoulder.

Continuing armhole shaping if necessary, work in patt until same length as back to shoulder. When all armhole shaping is complete, 6 sts remain. Fasten off.

Finishing

Sew side seams. Sew shoulder seams.

Neck Edging

With D, join yarn at right shoulder seam. Work 1 rnd sc around neck edge. Fasten off.

Armhole Edging

With D, join yarn at side seam. Work 1 rnd sc around armhole edge. Fasten off.

Weave in ends. Block lightly.

Portola

D elicate shell stitch crochet is enlivened with subtle stripes created by alternating regular and metallic versions of the same color. The simple shape lets your stitchwork shine.

SKILL LEVEL
Intermediate

SIZES
Women's Extra Small (Small, Medium, Large, Extra Large, 2X Large)

FINISHED MEASUREMENTS
Bust: $32^1/_4$ ($35^3/_4$, $39^1/_4$, $42^1/_2$, 46, $49^1/_2$)"/82 (91, 99.5, 108, 117, 125.5) cm

YARN
Nazli Gelin Garden 10, super fine weight #1 yarn (100% Egyptian Giza mercerized cotton; 306 yd./1.75 oz., 280 m/50 g per skein)
- 2 (2, 3, 3, 3, 3) skeins #700-27 Melon (A)

Nazli Gelin Garden 10 Metallic, super fine weight #1 yarn (99% Egyptian Giza mercerized cotton, 1% Lurex; 306 yd./1.75 oz., 280 m/50 g per skein)
- 2 (2, 3, 3, 3, 3) skeins #702-21 Melon with Orange (B)

HOOKS & NOTIONS
- US size D-3/3.25 mm crochet hook
- Tapestry needle

GAUGE
28 sts and 13 rows in Iris patt = 4"/10 cm

PATTERN NOTE
- Turning chain is counted as a st throughout.

STITCH PATTERN

Iris Pattern
Set-up row: Ch3 (counts as dc), sk first 2 sc, *(2 dc, ch1, 2 dc) in next sc, sk next 3 sc; rep from * to end, ending with, sk 1 sc, dc in last sc.
Row 1: Ch3, sk first 3 dc, *(2 dc, ch1, 2 dc) in ch-1 sp, sk next 4 dc; rep from * to last 2 dc, sk last 2 dc, dc in 3rd ch of beginning ch-3.
Rep Row 1 for patt.

Back

With A, ch 114 (126, 138, 150, 162, 174).

Row 1 (RS): Sc in 2nd ch from hook, sc in each ch to end. 113 (125, 137, 149, 161, 173) sts.

Row 2 (WS): Ch1, sk first sc, sc in each sc to end.

Begin working Iris patt.

Work Set-up row and Row 1 of patt.

Change to B.

Work Row 1 of patt twice.

Change to A.

Work Row 1 of patt twice.

Continue in patt, changing color every 2 rows, until piece measures 12 1/2"/32 cm, ending with a WS row.

Shape Armholes

NOTE: Continue to change colors in pattern throughout shaping.

Row 1: Work in patt to last 12 (12, 16, 16, 20, 20) dc, dc2 in next ch-1 sp, turn.

Row 2: Ch3, (dc2, ch1, dc2) in each ch-1 sp to last 12 (12, 16, 16, 20, 20) dc, 2 dc in next ch-1 sp, turn.

Row 3: Ch3, (dc2, ch1, dc2) in each ch-1 sp to last ch-1 sp, 2 dc in last ch-1 sp, turn.

Rep [Row 3] 0 (1, 1, 2, 2, 3) more times. 85 (89, 93, 97, 101, 105) sts.

Work even in patt until armhole measures 6 1/4 (6 3/4, 7 1/4, 7 3/4, 8 1/4, 8 3/4)"/16 (17, 18.5, 19, 20.5, 22) cm, ending with a WS row.

Shape Right Back Neck

Row 1 (RS): Ch3, (dc2, ch1, dc2) in next 5 (5, 6, 6, 6, 6) ch-1 sps, 2 dc in next ch-1 sp, turn.

Row 2 (WS): Ch3, (dc2, ch1, dc2) in each ch-1 sp, end dc in 3rd ch of beginning ch-3.

Row 3: Ch3, (dc2, ch1, dc2) in next 4 (4, 5, 5, 5, 5) ch-1 sps, 2 dc in last ch-1 sp, turn.

Row 4: Ch3, (dc2, ch1, dc2) in each ch-1 sp, end dc in 3rd ch of beginning ch-3. 17 (17, 21, 21, 21, 21) sts.

Work 2 rows even in patt.

Fasten off.

Shape Left Back Neck

With RS facing, rejoin yarn in 6th (6th, 7th, 7th, 7th, 7th) ch-1 sp from end of row.

Row 1 (RS): Ch3, (dc2, ch1, dc2) in next 5 (5, 6, 6, 6, 6) ch-1 sps, dc in 3rd ch of beginning ch-3.

Row 2 (WS): Ch3, (dc2, ch1, dc2) in next 4 (4, 5, 5, 5, 5) ch-1 sps, 2 dc in last ch-1 sp, turn.

Row 3: Ch3, (dc2, ch1, dc2) in next 4 (4, 5, 5, 5, 5) ch-1 sps, dc in 3rd ch of beginning ch-3.

Row 4: Ch3, (dc2, ch1, dc2) in each ch-1 sp, end dc in 3rd ch of beginning ch-3. 17 (17, 21, 21, 21, 21) sts.

Work 2 rows even in patt.

Fasten off.

Front

Work same as back until armhole measures 4"/10 cm.

Shape Left Front Neck

Row 1 (RS): Ch3, (dc2, ch1, dc2) in next 5 (5, 6, 6, 6, 6) ch-1 sps, 2 dc in next ch-1 sp, turn.

Row 2 (WS): Ch3, (dc2, ch1, dc2) in each ch-1 sp, end dc in 3rd ch of beginning ch-3.

Row 3: Ch3, (dc2, ch1, dc2) in next 4 (4, 5, 5, 5, 5) ch-1 sps, 2 dc in last ch-1 sp, turn.

Row 4: Ch3, (dc2, ch1, dc2) in each ch-1 sp, end dc in 3rd ch of beginning ch-3. 17 (17, 21, 21, 21, 21) sts.

Work 10 rows even in patt.

Fasten off.

Shape Right Front Neck

With RS facing, rejoin yarn in 6th (6th, 7th, 7th, 7th, 7th) ch-1 sp from end of row.

Row 1 (RS): Ch3, (dc2, ch1, dc2) in next 5 (5, 6, 6, 6, 6) ch-1 sps, dc in 3rd ch of beginning ch-3.

Row 2 (WS): Ch3, (dc2, ch1, dc2) in next 4 (4, 5, 5, 5, 5) ch-1 sps, 2 dc in last ch-1 sp, turn.

Row 3: Ch3, (dc2, ch1, dc2) in next 4 (4, 5, 5, 5, 5) ch-1 sps, dc in 3rd ch of beginning ch-3.

Row 4: Ch3, (dc2, ch1, dc2) in each ch-1 sp, end dc in 3rd ch of beginning ch-3. 17 (17, 21, 21, 21, 21) sts.

Work 10 rows even in patt.

Fasten off.

Finishing

Sew side seams. Sew shoulder seams.

Neck Edging

Join yarn at right shoulder seam. Work 1 rnd sc around neck edge.

Armhole Edging

Join yarn at side seam. Work 1 rnd sc around armhole edge. Fasten off.

Weave in ends. Block lightly.

Potrero

A ladylike and office-appropriate boat-neck shell needs little embellishment. The simple herringbone variation on half double crochet creates an intriguing texture.

SKILL LEVEL
Easy

SIZES
Women's Extra Small (Small, Medium, Large, Extra Large)

FINISHED MEASUREMENTS
Bust: 32 (35³/₄, 40¹/₂, 44¹/₂, 48)"/81.5 (91, 103, 113, 122) cm

YARN
Premier Yarns Deborah Norville Collection Cotton Soft Silk, medium weight #4 yarn (78% cotton, 22% silk; 154 yd./ 3 oz., 140 m/85 g per skein)
- 4 (4, 5, 6, 6) skeins #9508 Powder Blue

HOOKS & NOTIONS
- US size I-9/5.5 mm crochet hook
- Tapestry needle

GAUGE
13 sts and 11 rows in Herringbone Half Double Crochet = 4"/10 cm

PATTERN NOTES
- Back and Front are worked the same.
- Turning chain is counted as a stitch throughout.
- See page 89 for a photo tutorial on Herringbone Half Double Crochet.

SPECIAL STITCHES
Herringbone Half Double Crochet (Hbhdc): Yo, insert hook into next st, yo and pull through both the st and the first loop on the hook, yo and draw through both loops on hook. For a photo tutorial, see page 89.
Hbhdc2tog: Yo, insert hook into next st, yo and pull through both the st and the first loop on the hook, yo, insert hook into next st, yo and pull through both the st and the first loop on the hook, yo and draw through all 3 loops on hook.

Back

Ch 53 (59, 67, 73, 79).

Row 1 (RS): Hbhdc in 3rd ch from hook and in each ch to end. 52 (58, 66, 72, 78) sts.

Row 2 (WS): Ch2 (counts as a st), sk first st, Hbhdc in next st and in each st to end, working last Hbhdc in top of turning ch.

Rep Row 2 for patt.

Work even in Herringbone Half Double Crochet until piece measures 4 (4, 4^1/$_2$, 4^1/$_2$, 5)"/10 (10, 11.5, 11.5, 12.5) cm, ending with a WS row.

Shape Waist

Row 1 (Dec row) (RS): Ch2, sk first st, Hbhdc2tog in second and third sts, Hbhdc to last 2 sts, Hbhdc2tog in last 2 sts, Hbhdc in top of turning ch. 2 sts dec.

Rep Dec row every RS row 2 more times. 46 (52, 60, 66, 72) sts.

Work 3 rows even.

Next row (Inc row) (RS): Ch2, sk first st, 2Hbhdc in next st, Hbhdc to last st, 2Hbhdc in last st, Hbhdc in top of turning ch. 2 sts inc.

Rep Inc row every RS row 2 more times. 52 (58, 66, 72, 78) sts.

Work even in patt until piece measures 14^1/$_2$ (15, 15^1/$_2$, 16, 16^1/$_2$)"/37 (38, 39.5, 40.5, 42) cm, ending with a WS row and ending last row 3 (3, 4, 5, 6) sts before end.

Shape Armholes

Row 1 (RS): Ch2, sk first st, Hbhdc in next st and in each st to last 3 (3, 4, 5, 6) sts.

Row 2 (Dec row) (WS): Ch2, sk first st, Hbhdc2tog in second and third sts, Hbhdc to last 2 sts, Hbhdc2tog in last 2 sts, Hbhdc in top of turning ch. 2 sts dec.

Rep Dec row every row 1 (3, 5, 6, 7) more times. 42 (44, 46, 48, 50) sts.

Work even until armholes measure 5^3/$_4$ (6^1/$_4$, 6^3/$_4$, 7^1/$_4$, 7^3/$_4$)"/14.5 (16, 17, 18.5, 19.5) cm, ending with a WS row.

Shape Neck

Row 1 (RS): Ch2, sk first st, Hbhdc in next 5 (6, 6, 6, 6) sts, Hbhdc2tog over next 2 sts, Hbhdc in next st, turn work.

Continue on these 8 (9, 9, 9, 9) sts only.

Row 2 (WS): Ch2, sk first st, Hbhdc2tog in 2nd and 3rd sts, Hbhdc to last st, Hbhdc in top of turning ch. 7 (8, 8, 8, 8) sts. Fasten off.

Sk 24 (24, 26, 28, 30) sts at center neck and rejoin yarn.

Row 1 (RS): Ch2, sk first st, Hbhdc2tog in second and third sts, Hbhdc to last st, Hbhdc in top of turning ch. 8 (9, 9, 9, 9) sts.

(continued)

Row 2 (WS): Ch2, sk first st, Hbhdc in each st to last 2 sts, Hbhdc2tog over next 2 sts, Hbhdc in top of turning ch. 7 (8, 8, 8, 8) sts. Fasten off.

Front

Work same as for Back.

Finishing

Sew side seams. Sew shoulder seams.

Neck Edging

Join yarn at right shoulder seam. Work 1 rnd sc around neck edge. Work 1 rnd reverse sc around neck edge. Fasten off.

Armhole Edging

Join yarn at side seam. Work 1 rnd sc around armhole edge. Work 1 rnd reverse sc around armhole edge. Fasten off.

Weave in ends. Block lightly.

Sansome

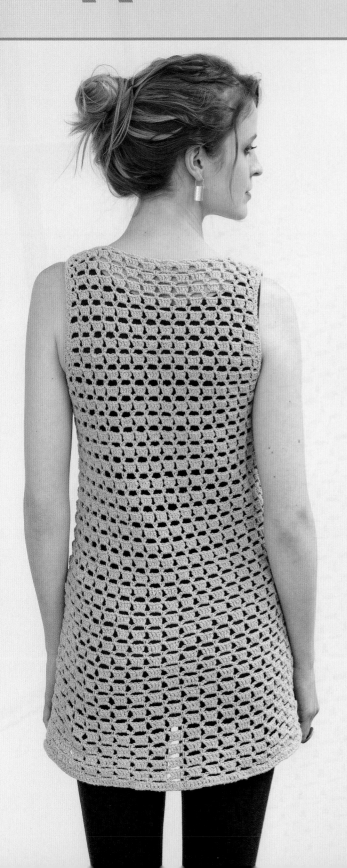

With its deep, buttoned front opening, this tunic is a sleek and versatile layering piece. The open stitch pattern creates a modern craft feeling.

SKILL LEVEL
Easy

SIZES
Women's Extra Small (Small, Medium, Large, Extra Large)

FINISHED MEASUREMENTS
Bust: 32³/₄ (36¹/₄, 40, 43¹/₂, 47¹/₄)"/83 (92, 101.5, 110.5, 120) cm

YARN
Kollage Yarns Riveting Sport, light weight #3 yarn (95% cotton, 5% other; 350 yd./3.5 oz., 320 m/100 g per skein)
- 3 (3, 3, 4, 4) skeins #7906 Cloud Denim

HOOKS & NOTIONS
- US size G-6/4.25 mm crochet hook
- Tapestry needle
- 8 buttons ¹/₂"/13 mm diameter
- Stitch marker

GAUGE
22 sts and 11 rows in Double Crochet Grid patt = 4"/10 cm

PATTERN NOTE
- Turning chain is not included in stitch counts.

STITCH PATTERN

Double Crochet Grid Pattern
Row 1 (WS): Ch1, sc in first dc, *ch4, sk 4 dc, sc in next dc; rep from * to end.
Row 2 (RS): Ch3, *dc4 in ch-4 sp, ch1; rep from * to end, ending with dc4 in ch-4 sp, dc in last sc.
Row 3: Ch1, sc in first dc, *ch4, sc in ch-1 sp; rep from * to end, ending with sc in 3rd ch of beginning ch-3.
Rep Rows 2–3 for patt.

Back

Ch 93 (103, 113, 123, 133).
Foundation row (WS): Dc in 4th ch from hook and in each ch to end. 90 (100, 110, 120, 130) dc.
Begin working Double Crochet Grid patt.
Work even in patt until piece measures 20"/51 cm, ending with a RS row.

Shape Armholes

Row 1 (WS): Ch1, sl st in each st to 3rd (3rd, 3rd, 4th, 4th) ch-1 sp, sc in ch-1 sp, work in patt until 3 (3, 3, 4, 4) ch-1 sps remain, sc in 3rd (3rd, 3rd, 4th, 4th) ch-1 sp from end, turn.
Row 2 (Dec row) (RS): Ch3, dc2tog in ch-4 sp, dc2 in same ch-4 sp, *ch1, dc4 in ch-4 sp; rep from * to last ch-4 sp, dc2 in ch-4 sp, dc2tog in ch-4 sp, dc in last sc. 2 sts dec.
Row 3: Ch1, sc in first dc, ch3, sc in ch-1 sp, *ch4, sc in ch-1 sp; rep from * to end, ending with ch 3, sc in 3rd ch of beginning ch-3.
Row 4 (Dec row): Ch3, dc2tog in ch-3 sp, dc2 in same ch-3 sp, *ch1, dc4 in ch-4 sp; rep from * to last ch-3 sp, dc in ch-3 sp, dc2tog in ch-3 sp, dc in last sc. 2 sts dec.
Row 5: Ch1, sc in first dc, ch2, sc in ch-1 sp, *ch4, sc in ch-1 sp; rep from * to end, ending with ch 2, sc in 3rd ch of beginning ch-3.
Continue in this manner, decreasing 1 st at beginning and end of every RS row 2 (5, 8, 5, 7) more times. 62 (66, 70, 76, 82) sts.
Work even in patt until armhole measures 7$\frac{1}{2}$ (8, 8$\frac{1}{2}$, 9, 9$\frac{1}{2}$)"/19 (20.5, 21.5, 23, 24) cm, ending with a WS row.

Shape Back Neck

Next row (RS): Ch3, work next 12 (13, 13, 15, 17) sts in patt, ending with dc.
Fasten off.
Sk center 38 (40, 44, 46, 48 sts), rejoin yarn. Ch3, work in patt to end.
Fasten off.

Front

Work same as for Back until piece measures 15"/38 cm, ending with a RS row.
Mark center ch-1 sp.

Right Front

Next row (WS): Work in patt to marked ch-1 sp, sc in marked sp, turn.
Continue in patt over these 45 (50, 55, 60, 65) sts until same length as back to armhole, ending with a RS row.

Shape Armhole

Next row (WS): Ch1, sl st in each st to 3rd (3rd, 3rd, 4th, 4th) ch-1 sp, sc in ch-1 sp, work in patt to end.
Shape armhole same as for back, decreasing at end of RS rows. 31 (33, 35, 38, 41) sts rem.
Work even until armhole measures 5$\frac{1}{2}$ (6, 6$\frac{1}{2}$, 7, 7$\frac{1}{2}$)"/14 (15, 16.5, 17.5, 19) cm, ending with a RS row.

Shape Neck

Next row (WS): Work 12 (13, 13, 15, 17) sts in patt, ending with sc, turn.
Continue in patt over these sts until same length as back to shoulder.
Fasten off.

Left Front

With WS facing, rejoin yarn in center ch-1 sp.
Next row (WS): Ch5 (counts as sc1, ch4), sc in ch-1 sp, continue in patt to end.
Continue in patt over these 45 (50, 55, 60, 65) sts until same length as back to armhole, ending with a RS row.

Shape Armhole

Next row (WS): Work in patt until 3 (3, 3, 4, 4) ch-1 sps remain, sc in 3rd (3rd, 3rd, 4th, 4th) ch-1 sp from end, turn.
Shape armhole same as for back, decreasing at beginning of RS rows. 31 (33, 35, 38, 41) sts rem.
Work even until armhole measures 5$\frac{1}{2}$ (6, 6$\frac{1}{2}$, 7, 7$\frac{1}{2}$)"/14 (15, 16.5, 17.5, 19) cm, ending with a RS row.

Shape Neck

Next row (WS): Ch1, sl st over first 19 (20, 22, 23, 24) sts, ch1, work in patt to end.
Continue in patt over these sts until same length as back to shoulder.
Fasten off.

Finishing

Sew side seams. Sew shoulder seams.

Neck Edging

Mark position of 8 button loops evenly spaced along right edge of front slit.

Join yarn at right shoulder seam. Work 1 rnd sc around neck edge, working 3 sc in each corner of front neck and sc2tog at bottom of front slit. At each marked button loop position, ch4 for button loop. Fasten off.

Armhole Edging

Join yarn at side seam. Work 1 rnd sc around armhole edge.

Fasten off.

Sew buttons to left edge of front slit to correspond with buttonholes.

Weave in ends. Block.

Mission

For many people, crochet equals granny squares. Pairing this classic motif with an eccentric stripe pattern in fresh citrus colors makes for an easy tank that will brighten your day.

SKILL LEVEL
Intermediate

SIZES
Women's Extra Small (Small, Medium, Large, Extra Large)

FINISHED MEASUREMENTS
Bust: 34 (37^1/$_4$, 40^1/$_2$, 43^3/$_4$, 47)"/86.5 (95, 103, 111, 119) cm

YARN
Bernat Cotton-ish by Vickie Howell, light weight #3 yarn (55% cotton, 45% acrylic; 282 yd./2.4 oz., 258 m/70 g per skein)
- 1 (1, 2, 2, 2) skeins #85620 Lemon Twill (A)
- 1 (1, 2, 2, 2) skeins #85416 Cotton Candy (B)
- 1 (1, 2, 2, 2) skeins #85628 Cotton Harvest (C)
- 1 (1, 2, 2, 2) skeins #85008 Cotton Ball (D)

HOOKS & NOTIONS
- US size G-6/4 mm crochet hook
- US size H-8/5 mm crochet hook
- Tapestry needle

GAUGE
15 sts and 8 rows in dc using larger hook = 4"/10 cm
Squares measure 2^1/$_2$"/6 cm on each side.

STRIPE SEQUENCE
1 row C. *Start back with this row.*
1 row B.
1 row D.
1 row A. *Start front with this row.*
1 row C.
1 row D.
1 row B.
1 row A.
1 row D.
Rep these 9 rows for Stripe Sequence.

Square A (make 8)

Using smaller hook and A, ch4, join with a sl st to form ring.

Rnd 1: Ch3 (counts as dc), dc2 into ring, ch1, *dc3, ch1; rep from * 2 more times, join to top of ch3 with sl st. Fasten off.

Rnd 2: Join B in any ch-1 sp, ch3 (counts as dc), [dc2, ch1, dc3] into same ch-1 sp, ch1,*[dc3, ch1, dc3] in next ch-1 sp, ch1; rep from * 2 more times, join to top of ch3 with sl st. Fasten off.

Rnd 3: Join D in any ch-1 corner sp, ch3 (counts as dc), [dc2, ch1, dc3] into same ch-1 sp, dc3 in next sp, *[dc3, ch1, dc3] in next ch-1 corner sp, dc3 in next sp; rep from * 2 more times, join to top of ch3 with sl st. Fasten off.

Square B (make 8)

Make same as Square A, but use C for Rnd 2 instead of B.

Assemble Yoke

Arrange 2 of Square A and 3 of Square B into a strip, beginning and ending with Square B and alternating colors. Sew together using a whipstitch and butting sides of squares together.

Make another strip in the same way.

Arrange remaining squares into 2 strips 3 squares long, each beginning and ending with Square A and with Square B in the middle. Sew together.

Arrange strips into the four sides of a square, with Square B in each corner. Sew together.

Back

Using smaller hook, join D to one outer corner of yoke.

Row 1 (RS): With RS facing, ch1, sc 50 along edge of one side of yoke (about 10 sts in each square). Fasten off.

Change to larger hook and C.

Begin working in Stripe Sequence, and continue throughout.

Row 2 (WS): Ch3, dc in second sc and in each sc, ending with dc in top of ch1.

Row 3: Ch 3, dc in second dc and in each dc, ending with dc in top of ch3.

Rep Row 3 for patt.

After 3rd (3rd, 4th, 5th, 5th) row of Stripe Sequence, begin armhole shaping.

Shape Armholes

With next color in sequence, ch 7 (10, 13, 16, 19). Fasten off and set ch aside.

Next row: Join next color in sequence, ch 9 (12, 15, 18, 21), dc in 4th ch from hook and in each rem ch, work in patt across dc of previous row, dc in each st of ch made earlier. 64 (70, 76, 82, 88) dc.

Continue working in Stripe Sequence and patt until piece measures 16"/40.5 cm below yoke. Fasten off.

Front

Using smaller hook, join D to one outer corner of yoke.

Row 1 (RS): With RS facing, ch1, sc 50 along edge of one side of yoke (about 10 sts in each square). Fasten off.

Sizes Extra Small and Small ONLY

Shape Armholes

Change to larger hook and A.

Ch 7 (10, -, -, -). Fasten off and set ch aside.

Row 2 (WS): Join A. Ch9 (12, -, -, -), dc in 4th ch from hook and in each rem ch, dc in each sc of previous row, dc in each st of ch made earlier. 64 (70, -, -, -) dc.

Row 3: With next color in Stripe Sequence, ch3, dc in second dc and in each dc, ending with dc in top of ch3.

Continue as for back.

Size Medium ONLY

Change to larger hook and A.

Begin working in Stripe Sequence, and continue throughout.

Row 2 (WS): Ch3, dc in second sc and in each sc, ending with dc in top of ch1.

Shape Armholes

With C, ch - (-, 13, -, -). Fasten off and set ch aside.

Row 3 (RS): Join C, ch - (-, 15, -, -), dc in 4th ch from hook and in each rem ch, work in patt across dc of previous row, dc in each st of ch made earlier. - (-, 76, -, -) dc.

Row 4: With next color in Stripe Sequence, ch3, dc in second dc and in each dc, ending with dc in top of ch3.

Continue as for back.

Sizes Large and Extra Large ONLY

Change to larger hook and A.
Begin working in Stripe Sequence, and continue
   throughout.
Row 2 (WS): Ch3, dc in second sc and in each sc, ending
   with dc in top of ch1.
Row 3 (RS): Ch3, dc in second dc and in each dc, ending
   with dc in top of ch3.

Shape Armholes

With D, ch - (-, -, 16, 19). Fasten off and set ch aside.
Row 4 (WS): Join D, ch - (-, -, 18, 21), dc in 4th ch from hook
   and in each rem ch, work in patt across dc of previous
   row, dc in each st of ch made earlier. - (-, -, 82, 88) dc.
Row 5: With next color in Stripe Sequence, ch3, dc in
   second dc and in each dc, ending with dc in top of ch3.
Continue as for back.

Finishing

Sew side seams.

Neck Edging

Join yarn at a back neck corner. Using smaller hook, work 1
   rnd sc around neckline, working sc2tog in each corner.

Armhole Edging

Join yarn at side seam. Using smaller hook, work 1 rnd sc
   around armhole.
Rep for other armhole.

Hem Edging

Join yarn at a side seam. Using smaller hook, work 1 rnd sc
   around lower edge.
Weave in ends. Block.

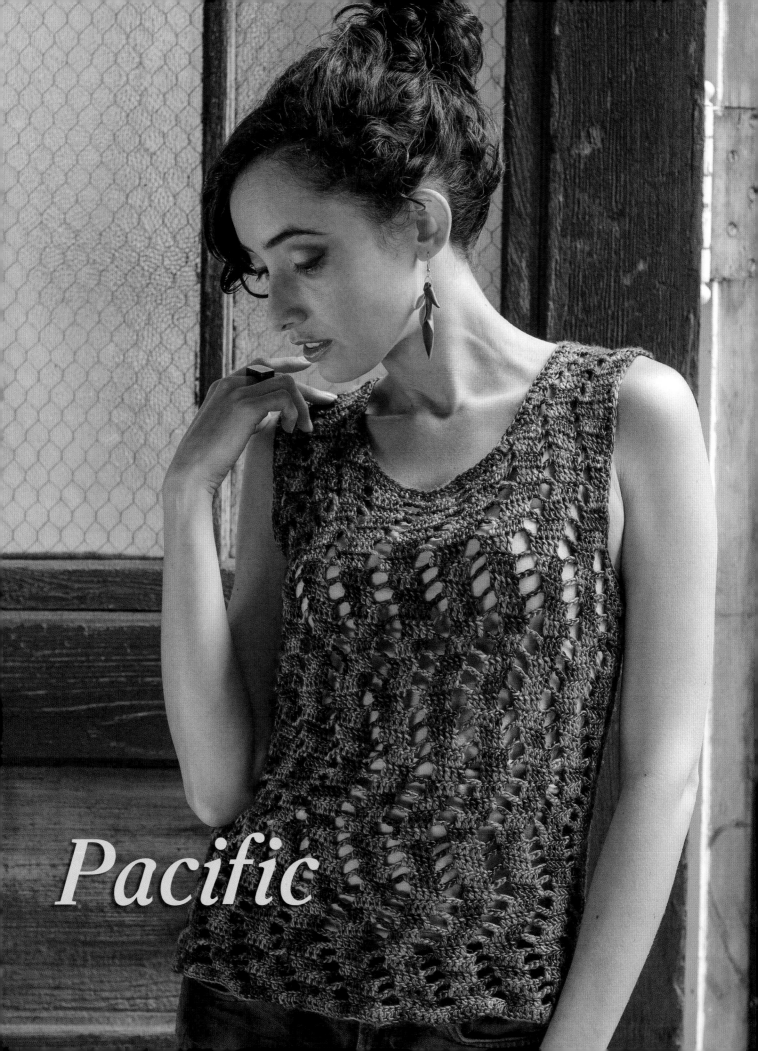

Pacific

The vertical waves in this openwork stitch pattern remind me of kelp swaying with the motion of the sea. The hand-dyed silk yarn makes this a luxury you'll love to wear.

SKILL LEVEL
Easy

SIZES
Women's Extra Small (Small, Medium, Large, Extra Large)

FINISHED MEASUREMENTS
Bust: 34³/₄ (38¹/₄, 41³/₄, 45¹/₄, 49)"/88.5 (97, 106, 115, 124.5) cm

YARN
LB Collection One Hundred Percent Silk, fine weight #2 yarn (100% silk; 163 yd./1.75 oz., 150 m/50 g per skein)
- 3 (3, 4, 4, 5) skeins #201 Gemini

HOOKS & NOTIONS
- US size H-8/5 mm crochet hook
- Tapestry needle

GAUGE
18 sts and 9 rows in hdc = 4"/10 cm

PATTERN NOTE
- Turning chain is included in stitch counts throughout.

STITCH PATTERN

Sliding Blocks Pattern

Row 1 (RS): Ch3, sk first dc, *dc in next 5 dc, ch3, sk next 3 dc; rep from * to end, ending with dc in last 3 dc, dc in 3rd ch of beginning ch-3.

Row 2 (WS): Ch3, sk first dc, dc in next 3 dc, *dc in ch-3 sp, ch3, sk next dc, dc in next 4 dc; rep from * to end, end with dc in 3rd ch of beginning ch-3.

Row 3: Ch3, sk first dc, dc in next 3 dc, *sk next dc, ch3, dc in ch-3 sp, dc in next 4 dc; rep from * to end, ending with dc in 3rd ch of beginning ch-3.

Row 4: Ch4, sk first 2 dc, *dc in next 4 dc, dc in ch-3 sp, ch3, sk next dc; rep from * to end, ending with dc in last 2 dc, dc in 3rd ch of beginning ch-3.

Row 5: Ch3, sk first dc, dc in next dc, *sk next dc, ch3, dc in ch-3 sp, dc in next 4 dc; rep from * to end, ending with sk next dc, ch2, dc in 3rd ch of beginning ch-4.

Row 6: Ch4, sk first 2 dc, dc in ch-2 sp, *dc in next 4 dc, sk next dc, ch3, dc in ch-3 sp; rep from * to end, ending dc in last dc, dc in 3rd ch of beginning ch-3.

Row 7: Ch3, sk first dc, dc in next 2 dc, *dc in ch-3 sp, ch3, sk next dc, dc in next 4 dc; rep from * to end, ending with dc in ch-4 sp, dc in 3rd ch of beginning ch-4.

Row 8: Ch3, sk first dc, *dc in next 4 dc, sk next dc, ch3, dc in ch-3 sp; rep from * to end, ending with dc in next 3 dc, dc in 3rd ch of beginning ch-3.

Row 9: Ch3, sk first dc, *dc in next 4 sts, dc in ch-3 sp, ch3, sk next dc; rep from * to end, ending with dc in last 3 dc, dc in 3rd ch of beginning ch-3.

Rep Rows 2–9 for patt.

Back

Ch 81 (89, 97, 105, 113).

Foundation row (WS): Dc in 4th ch from hook and in each ch to end. 78 (86, 94, 102, 110) sts.

Begin working Sliding Blocks patt.

Work even in patt until piece measures 13 (13, 13^1/$_2$, 14, 14^1/$_2$)"/3 (33, 34.5, 35.5, 37) cm, ending with a WS row.

Shape Armholes

Row 1 (RS): Ch1, sl st over next 3 (5, 7, 9, 11) sts, ch3, work in patt to last 3 (5, 7, 9, 11) sts, ending with dc, turn.

Row 2 (Dec row): Ch3, sk first dc, dc2tog over next 2 sts, work in patt to last 2 dc, dc2tog, dc in 3rd ch of beginning ch-3. 2 sts dec.

Rep Dec row every row 1 (2, 3, 4, 6) more times. 68 (70, 72, 74, 74) sts.

(continued)

Work even in patt until armhole measures 6$\frac{1}{2}$ (6$\frac{1}{2}$, 7, 7$\frac{1}{2}$, 8)"/16.5 (16.5, 18, 19, 20.5) cm, ending with a WS row.

Shape Back Neck

Next row (RS): Work in patt across first 12 (13, 14, 15, 15) sts, dc in next 2 sts. Fasten off.
Sk center 40 sts and rejoin yarn. Ch3, dc in next st, work in patt to end. Fasten off.

Front

Work same as for back until armholes measure 3"/7.5 cm, ending with a WS row.
Mark center 32 sts.

Left Front

Row 1 (RS): Work in patt to 3 sts before marked center sts, dc2tog, dc in next st, turn.
Row 2 (WS): Ch3, sk first dc, dc2tog, work in patt to end.
Rows 3–4: Rep Rows 1–2. 14 (15, 16, 17, 17) sts.
Work even until same length as back to shoulder. Fasten off.

Right Front

With RS facing, rejoin yarn at second marker.
Row 1 (RS): Ch3, sk first dc, dc2tog, work in patt to end.
Row 2 (WS): Work in patt to last 2 sts, dc2tog, dc in 3rd ch of beginning ch-3.
Rows 3–4: Rep Rows 1–2. 14 (15, 16, 17, 17) sts.
Work even until same length as back to shoulder. Fasten off.

Finishing

Sew side seams. Sew shoulder seams.

Neck Edging

Join yarn at right shoulder seam. Work 1 rnd dc around neck edge, working 3 dc in each ch-3 sp. Fasten off.

Armhole Edging

Join yarn at side seam. Work 1 rnd sc around armhole edge.
Fasten off.
Weave in ends. Block lightly.

Clipper

This simple camisole is easy to make and easy to wear. The stripes of cool colors on a bright white background keep the look light and fresh.

SKILL LEVEL
Easy

SIZES
Women's Extra Small (Small, Medium, Large, Extra Large)

FINISHED MEASUREMENTS
Bust: 31 (35, 39, 43, 47)"/78.5 (89, 99, 109, 119.5) cm

YARN
Premier Yarns Cotton Fair, fine weight #2 yarn (52% cotton, 48% acrylic; 317 yd./3.5 oz., 290 m/100 g per skein)
- 2 (2, 3, 3, 4) skeins #27-07 White (A)
- 1 skein #27-04 Turquoise (B)
- 1 skein #27-03 Baby Blue (C)
- 1 skein #27-10 Leaf Green (D)

HOOKS & NOTIONS
- US size G-6/4.5 mm crochet hook
- Tapestry needle

GAUGE
22 sts and 22 rows in Spotted Stripe patt = 4"/10 cm

PATTERN NOTE
- Break yarn at each color change.

STITCH PATTERN

Spotted Stripe Pattern
Row 1 (WS): With A, sc in first 2 sts, *ch1, sk1, sc in next sc; rep from * to end. Change to B, ch1, turn.
Row 2 (RS): With B, sc in first st, *sc in ch-1 sp, ch1, sk1; rep from * to last st, sc1. Change to A, ch1, turn.
Row 3: With A, sc in first 2 sts, *ch1, sk1, sc in next sc; rep from * to end, ch1, turn.
Row 4: With A, sc in each sc and ch-1 sp to end, ch1, turn.
Row 5: Rep Row 1, changing to C at the end.
Row 6: With C, rep Row 2.
Rows 7–8: Rep Rows 3–4.
Row 9: Rep Row 1, changing to D at the end.
Row 10: With D, rep Row 2.
Rows 11–12: Rep Rows 3–4.
Rep Rows 1–12 for patt.

Back

With A, ch 87 (97, 109, 119, 131).

Row 1 (RS): Sc in 2nd ch from hook and in each ch across, ch1, turn. 86 (96, 108, 118, 130) sts. Turning ch is not counted as a st.

Rows 2–3: Sc in each sc, ch 1, turn.

Work in Spotted Stripe patt until piece measures 14 (14$\frac{1}{2}$, 15, 15$\frac{1}{2}$, 16)"/35.5 (37, 38, 39.5, 40.5) cm, ending with a WS row.

Shape Armholes

Row 1 (RS): Sl st in first 6 (7, 8, 9, 10) sts, ch1, work in patt until 6 (7, 8, 9, 10) sts rem in row, ch1, turn leaving rem sts unworked.

Row 2 (WS): Work in patt to end of row, leaving slipped sts unworked. 74 (82, 92, 100, 110) sts.

Next 4 (4, 6, 8, 10) rows: Sl st in first 3 sts, work in patt to end. 62 (64, 68, 70, 74) sts.

Last row: With A, sc in each st to end. Fasten off.

Front

Work same as back until piece measures 14 (14$\frac{1}{2}$, 15, 15$\frac{1}{2}$, 16)"/35.5 (37, 38, 39.5, 40.5) cm, ending with a WS row.

Shape Armholes

Row 1 (RS): Sl st in first 6 (7, 8, 9, 10) sts, ch1, work in patt until 6 (7, 8, 9, 10) sts rem in row, ch1, turn leaving rem sts unworked.

Row 2 (WS): Work in patt to end of row, leaving slipped sts unworked. 74 (82, 92, 100, 110) sts.

Row 3 (Dec row): Sc2tog, work in patt to last 2 sts, sc2tog. 2 sts dec.

Rep Dec row every row 5 (8, 11, 14, 17) more times. 62 (64, 68, 70, 74) sts.

Work even in patt until armholes measure 3 (3$\frac{1}{4}$, 3$\frac{1}{2}$, 3$\frac{3}{4}$, 4)"/7.5 (8.5, 9, 9.5, 10) cm, ending with a RS row. Fasten off.

Finishing

Weave in ends. Sew side seams.

Shoulder Straps

Join A at upper left corner of front. Ch 42 (44, 46, 48, 50).

Before joining shoulder strap chain to back, try your camisole on to check the fit. Adjust the length of the chain if necessary.

Join strap to upper corner of left back with sl st.

Work 1 rnd sc around armhole edge, working into the bumps on the back of the shoulder strap ch. Fasten off.

Rep for right strap.

Neck Edging

Join A at left back neck corner. Work 2 rnds sc around neck edge, working sc2tog at each of the 2 front neck corners and back neck corners. Fasten off.

Weave in ends. Block lightly.

Greenwich

*T*he contrasting trim on the collar of this tank brings the focus to your face. The armholes are carved in a bit to show off pretty shoulders.

SKILL LEVEL
Easy

SIZES
Women's Extra Small (Small, Medium, Large, Extra Large)

FINISHED MEASUREMENTS
Bust: 31³/₄ (35¹/₄, 39³/₄, 43¹/₄, 47³/₄)"/80.5 (89.5, 100.5, 110, 121) cm

YARN
Bernat Cotton-ish by Vickie Howell, light weight #3 yarn (55% cotton, 45% acrylic; 282 yd./2.4 oz., 258 m/70 g per skein)
- 3 (4, 5, 5, 6) skeins #85012 Coffee Filter (MC)
- 1 skein #85008 Cotton Ball (CC)

HOOKS & NOTIONS
- US size G-6/4 mm crochet hook
- Tapestry needle

GAUGE
22 sts and 13 rows in Paired Half Double Crochet patt = 4"/10 cm

PATTERN NOTES
- Turning chain counts as a stitch throughout.
- See pages 87 and 88 for photo tutorials on hdc and hdc2tog.

STITCH PATTERN

Paired Half Double Crochet Pattern
Row 1: Ch2, hdc2tog over first and second ch sps, *ch1, hdc2tog by inserting hook in same ch sp as last st, then in next ch sp; rep from * working second leg of last hdc2tog under turning chain of previous row, ch 1, hdc in 2nd ch of turning ch.
Rep Row 1 for patt.

Back

With MC, ch 89 (99, 111, 121, 133).

Set-up row (RS): Hdc2tog over 3rd and 4th ch from hook, *ch1, hdc2tog over next 2 ch; rep from * to last ch, ch1, hdc in last ch. 88 (98, 110, 120, 132) sts.

Begin working Paired Half Double Crochet patt. Work even until piece measures 14$\frac{1}{2}$ (15, 15$\frac{1}{2}$, 16, 16$\frac{1}{2}$)"/37 (38, 39.5, 40.5, 42) cm, ending with a WS row.

Shape Armholes

Rows 1–2: Work in patt to last 4 (5, 6, 7, 8) sts, turn work.

Rows 3–4: Work in patt to last 2 (2, 3, 3, 3) sts, turn work.

Next row (Dec row): Ch2, hdc3tog over next 3 ch sps, *ch1, hdc2tog by inserting hook in same ch sp as last st, then in next ch sp; rep from * working second leg of last hdc2tog under turning chain of previous row, ch 1, hdc in 2nd ch of turning ch. 2 sts dec.

Rep Dec row every row 15 (17, 19, 21, 23) more times. 44 (48, 52, 58, 64) sts.

Work even until armhole measures 6$\frac{1}{2}$ (7, 7$\frac{1}{2}$, 8, 8$\frac{1}{2}$)"/16.5 (18, 19, 20.5, 21.5) cm.

Fasten off.

Front

Work same as Back until piece measures 14$\frac{1}{2}$ (15, 15$\frac{1}{2}$, 16, 16$\frac{1}{2}$)"/37 (38, 39.5, 40.5, 42) cm, ending with a WS row.

Shape Armholes and Front Neck

Rows 1–2: Work in patt to last 4 (5, 6, 7, 8) sts, turn work. Mark center of sts.

Row 3 (RS): Work in patt to marked center st, turn work. 40 (44, 49, 53, 58) sts. Continue on these sts only for left front.

Left Front

Row 1 (WS): Work in patt to last 2 (2, 3, 3, 3) sts, turn work. 38 (42, 46, 50, 55) sts.

Row 2 (Dec row) (RS): Ch2, hdc3tog over next 3 ch sps, *ch1, hdc2tog by inserting hook in same ch sp as last st, then in next ch sp; rep from * working 2nd leg of last hdc2tog under turning chain of previous row, ch 1, hdc in 2nd ch of turning ch. 2 sts dec.

Rep Row 2 every RS row (dec at armhole edge only) 4 (5, 6, 6, 7) more times. 28 (30, 32, 36, 39) sts.

Work 1 WS row even.

Next row (RS): Ch2, hdc3tog over next 3 ch sps, *ch1, hdc2tog by inserting hook in same ch sp as last st, then in next ch sp; rep from * to last 10 (12, 12, 16, 17) sts, turn work.

Next row (Dec row): Ch2, hdc3tog over next 3 ch sps, *ch1, hdc2tog by inserting hook in same ch sp as last st, then in next ch sp; rep from * working 2nd leg of last hdc2tog under turning chain of previous row, ch 1, hdc in 2nd ch of turning ch. 2 sts dec.

Rep Dec row every row 4 more times. 7 (7, 9, 9, 11) sts.

Work even until armhole measures 6$\frac{1}{2}$ (7, 7$\frac{1}{2}$, 8, 8$\frac{1}{2}$)"/16.5 (18, 19, 20.5, 21.5) cm.

Fasten off.

Right Front

Rejoin yarn at center front, in same space as last st of Left Front.

Row 1 (RS): Work in patt to last 2 (2, 3, 3, 3) sts, turn work. 38 (42, 46, 50, 55) sts.

Row 2 (Dec row) (WS): Ch2, hdc3tog over next 3 ch sps, *ch1, hdc2tog by inserting hook in same ch sp as last st, then in next ch sp; rep from * working 2nd leg of last hdc2tog under turning chain of previous row, ch 1, hdc in 2nd ch of turning ch. 2 sts dec.

Rep Row 2 every WS row (dec at armhole edge only) 4 (5, 6, 6, 7) more times. 28 (30, 32, 36, 39) sts.

Work 1 RS row even.

Next row (WS): Ch2, hdc3tog over next 3 ch sps, *ch1, hdc2tog by inserting hook in same ch sp as last st, then in next ch sp; rep from * to last 10 (12, 12, 16, 17) sts, turn work.

Next row (Dec row): Ch2, hdc3tog over next 3 ch sps, *ch1, hdc2tog by inserting hook in same ch sp as last st, then in next ch sp; rep from * working 2nd leg of last hdc2tog under turning chain of previous row, ch 1, hdc in 2nd ch of turning ch. 2 sts dec.

Rep Dec row every row 4 more times. 7 (7, 9, 9, 11) sts.

Work even until armhole measures 6½ (7, 7½, 8, 8½)"/16.5 (18, 19, 20.5, 21.5) cm.

Fasten off.

Finishing

Sew shoulder seams. Sew side seams.

Collar

Join MC at right front neck.

Row 1 (RS): Work in patt across sts at right front neck, work (ch1, hdc2tog) 6 times up side edge of front neck, work in patt across sts at back neck, work (ch1, hdc2tog) 6 times down side edge of front neck, work in patt across sts at left front neck. 64 (72, 72, 86, 90) sts.

Work 7 more rows in patt. Do not break yarn.

Collar Edging

With MC, ch1, sc in each st and ch sp across collar to last st, sc3 in corner st, sc down left front collar and neck edge to bottom of neck opening, sc3tog at bottom of neck opening, sc up right front neck edge and collar to corner, sc3 in corner st, break yarn.

With CC, join with sl st to turning ch of MC round, sc in each st to corner, sc3 in corner st, sc in each st to bottom of neck opening, sc3tog at bottom of neck opening, sc in each st to end of rnd, join with sl st and fasten off.

Armhole Edging

Join MC at side seam. Work 1 rnd of sc around armhole, break yarn.

With CC, join with sl st to turning ch of MC round, sc in each st around armhole, join with sl st and fasten off.

Weave in ends. Block lightly.

Taraval

The round yoke with its concentric rings of contrasting bobbles brings interest to a breezy smock shape. This tank is worked from the yoke down, so adjusting the length is easy.

SKILL LEVEL
Intermediate

SIZES
Women's Extra Small (Small, Medium, Large, Extra Large)

FINISHED MEASUREMENTS
Bust: 34 (38$\frac{1}{2}$, 42$\frac{1}{2}$, 47, 51)"/86.5 (98, 108, 119.5, 129.5) cm

YARN
Premier Yarns Cotton Fair, fine weight #2 yarn (52% cotton, 48% acrylic; 317 yd./3.5 oz., 290 m/100 g per skein)
- 2 (2, 3, 3, 4) skeins #27-01 White (A)
- 1 skein #27-08 Red (B)

HOOKS & NOTIONS
- US size G-6/4 mm crochet hook
- Tapestry needle

GAUGE
15 sts and 12 rows in Alternating Rows patt = 4"/10 cm

PATTERN NOTE
- Turning chain is included in stitch counts throughout.

STITCH PATTERN

Alternating Rows Pattern
Row 1 (RS): Ch3, sk first sc, dc in each sc to end, ending with dc in beginning ch-1.
Row 2 (WS): Ch1, sk first dc, sc in each dc to end, ending with sc in 3rd ch of beginning ch-3.
Rep Rows 1–2 for patt.

Yoke

With A, ch 111.

Row 1 (RS): Sc in 2nd ch from hook and in each ch to end. 110 sts.

Rows 2–3: Ch1, sc in each sc to end.

Change to B.

Row 4 (WS): Ch1, *sc in next 2 sc, dc5tog in next sc, sc in next 2 sc; rep from * to end. 22 bobbles.

Change to A.

Row 5: Ch1, sc in each st to end.

Row 6 (Inc row): Ch1, *sc in next 2 sc, sc2 in next sc, sc in 2 sc; rep from * to end. 132 sts.

Row 7: Ch1, sc in each st to end.

Change to B.

Row 8: Ch1, *sc in next 2 sc, dc5tog in next sc, sc in next 3 sc; rep from * to end.

Change to A.

Row 9: Ch1, sc in each st to end.

Row 10 (Inc row): Ch1, *sc in next 3 sc, sc2 in next sc, sc in 2 sc; rep from * to end. 154 sts.

Row 11: Ch1, sc in each st to end.

Change to B.

Row 12: Ch1, *sc in next 3 sc, dc5tog in next sc, sc in next 3 sc; rep from * to end.

Change to A.

Row 13: Ch1, sc in each st to end.

Row 14 (Inc row): Ch1, *sc in next 3 sc, sc2 in next sc, sc in 3 sc; rep from * to end. 176 sts.

Row 15: Ch1, sc in each st to end.

Change to B.

Row 16: Ch1, *sc in next 3 sc, dc5tog in next sc, sc in next 4 sc; rep from * to end.

Change to A.

Row 17: Ch1, sc in each st to end.

Row 18 (Inc row): Ch1, *sc in next 4 sc, sc2 in next sc, sc in 3 sc; rep from * to end. 198 sts.

Row 19: Ch1, sc in each st to end.

Fasten off.

Sew ends of yoke together to form a ring.

Back

With RS facing, join A at seam.

Size Extra Small Only

Row 1 (RS): Ch3, working in back loop only *dc in next 2 sc, dc2 in next sc; rep from * 15 more times. 64 dc.

Size Small Only

Row 1 (RS): Ch3, working in back loop only *dc in next sc, dc2 in next sc; rep from * 23 more times. 72 dc.

Size Medium Only

Row 1 (RS): Ch3, working in back loop only *dc in next sc, dc2 in next 2 sc; rep from * 15 more times. 80 dc.

Size Large Only

Row 1 (RS): Ch3, working in back loop only *dc in next sc, dc2 in next 5 sc; rep from * 7 more times. 88 dc.

Size Extra Large Only

Row 1 (RS): Ch3, working in back loop only dc2 in next 48 sc. 96 dc.

All sizes

Row 2 (WS): Ch1, sc in each dc to end.

Begin working Alternating Rows patt.

Work even in patt until back measures 16 (16, 17, 18, 19)"/40.5 (40.5, 43, 45.5, 48.5) cm from yoke, ending with Row 2 of patt.

Next 2 rows: Ch1, sc in each sc to end.

Fasten off.

Front

With RS facing, sk 51 sc from last st of back on yoke edge. Join A.

Work same as for back until front measures 13 (13, 14, 15, 16)"/33 (33, 35.5, 38, 40.5) cm from yoke, ending with Row 2 of patt.

Next 2 rows: Ch1, sc in each sc to end.

Fasten off.

Finishing

Sew side seams, beginning at lower edge and ending $3^1/2$ (4, $4^1/2$, 5, $5^1/2$)"/9 (10, 11.5, 12.5, 14) cm below the point where front meets yoke.

Weave in ends. Block lightly.

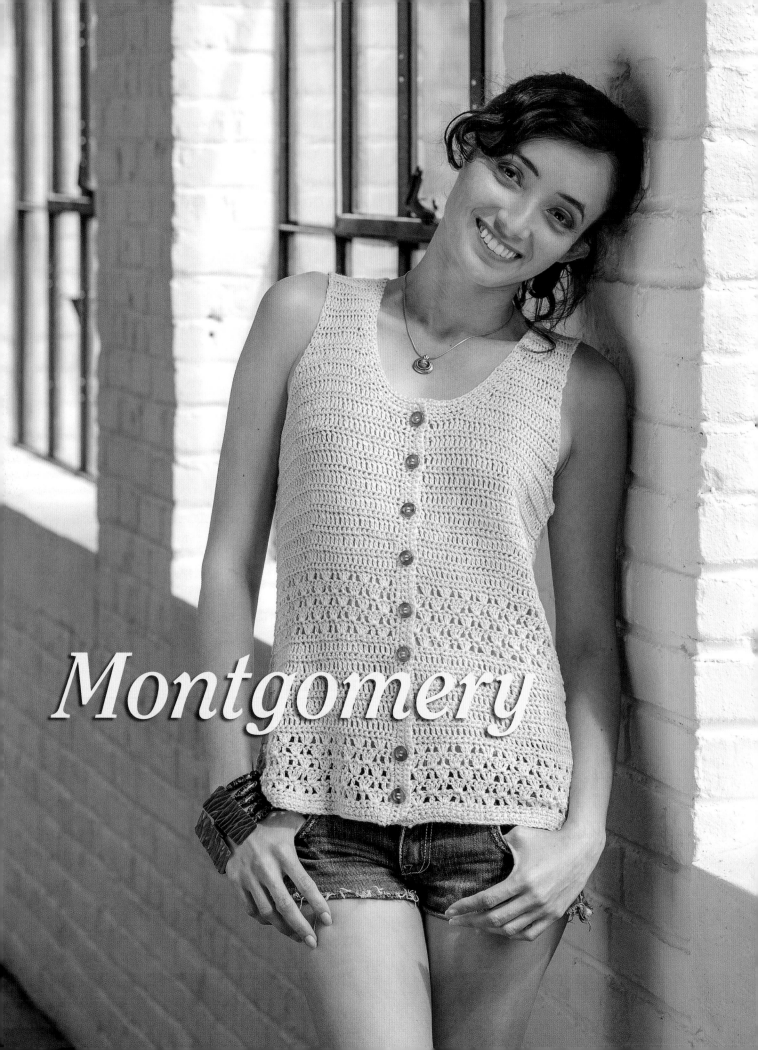

Montgomery

T his button-front tank works well both layered and on its own. The shaped waist and bands of open stitchwork flatter just about any figure.

SKILL LEVEL
Intermediate

SIZES
Women's Extra Small (Small, Medium, Large, Extra Large)

FINISHED MEASUREMENTS
Bust: 33 (36³/₄, 40¹/₂, 44¹/₄, 48)"/84 (93.5, 103, 112.5, 122) cm

YARN
Fibra Natura Flax, light weight #3 yarn (100% linen; 137 yd./1.75 oz., 125 m/50 g per skein)
- 5 (5, 6, 6, 7) skeins #101 Buttercream

HOOKS & NOTIONS
- US size G-6/4 mm crochet hook
- Locking stitch markers
- Tapestry needle
- 9 buttons, ⁵/₈"/15 mm diameter

GAUGE
17 sts and 14 rows in Alternating Stripe patt = 4"/10 cm
17 sts and 10 rows in V-stitch patt = 4"/10 cm

PATTERN NOTES
- Turning chain is not included in stitch counts.
- See page 91 for a photo tutorial on dc2tog.

STITCH PATTERNS

Alternating Stripe Pattern
Row 1 (WS): Ch1, sc in each st to end.
Row 2 (RS): Ch3, dc in each st to end.
Rep Rows 1–2 for patt.

V-Stitch Pattern
Rows 1, 3, and 5 (RS): Ch3, *dc in first st, sk 1, dc3 in next st, sk 1; rep from * to last st, dc in last st.
Rows 2 and 4 (WS): Ch3, dc2 in first st, *sk 1, dc in next st, sk 1, dc3 in next st; rep from * to last 4 sts, sk 1, dc in next st, sk 1, dc2 in last st.

Body

Ch 138 (154, 170, 186, 202).

Row 1 (RS): Sc in 2nd ch from hook and in each ch to end. 137 (153, 169, 185, 201) sts.

Rows 2–4: Ch 1, sc in each st to end.

Work 5 rows of V-Stitch patt.

Begin working Alternating Stripe patt. Work even until piece measures 4"/10 cm, ending with a WS row.

Shape Waist

Place shaping markers on each side of center 35 (39, 43, 47, 51) sts and 17 (19, 21, 23, 25) sts away from each end. 4 markers total.

Next row (Dec row) (RS): Work in patt to first marker, dc2tog, work in patt to 2 sts before second marker, dc2tog, work in patt to third marker, dc2tog, work in patt to 2 sts before last marker, dc2tog, work in patt to end. 4 sts dec. Move markers up to current row as you work.

Rep Dec row every RS row 3 more times.

Work 1 WS row even in Alternating Stripe patt.

Work 5 rows of V-Stitch patt.

Work Row 1 of Alternating Stripe patt.

Check placement of markers on each side of center 35 (39, 43, 47, 51) sts, and 17 (19, 21, 23, 25) sts away from each end. 4 markers total.

Work remainder of piece in Alternating Stripe patt.

Next row (Inc row) (RS): Work in patt to first marker, dc2 in next st, work in patt to 1 st before second marker, dc2 in next st, work in patt to third marker, dc2 in next st, work in patt to 1 st before last marker, dc2 in next st, work in patt to end. 4 sts inc. Move markers up to current row as you work.

Rep Inc row every RS row 3 more times. 137 (153, 169, 185, 201) sts.

Work even in patt until piece measures 15"/38 cm, ending with a WS row.

Divide for Armholes

Next row (RS): Ch3, dc in next 28 (31, 34, 37, 40) sts, hdc in next st, sc in next st, sl st in next 8 (10, 12, 14, 16) sts, sc in next st, hdc in next st, dc in next 57 (63, 69, 75, 81) sts, hdc in next st, sc in next st, sl st in next 8 (10, 12, 14, 16) sts, sc in next st, hdc in next st, dc in next st and in each st to end.

Continue on 28 (31, 34, 37, 40) left front dcs only.

Left Front

Row 1 (WS): Ch1, sc in each st to end.

Shape Armhole and Front Neck

Row 2 (RS): Ch3, dc2tog, dc in next 20 (22, 24, 26, 28) sts, dc2tog, turn work. 22 (24, 26, 28, 30) sts.

Row 3: Ch1, sc in each st to end.

Row 4 (Dec row): Ch3, dc2tog, dc to last 2 sts, dc2tog. 2 sts dec.

Rep Dec row every RS row 3 (4, 5, 5, 6) more times. 14 (14, 14, 16, 16) sts.

Next row (Neck Edge Dec row) (RS): Ch3, dc in each st to last 2 sts, dc2tog. 1 st dec.

Rep Neck Edge Dec row every RS row 2 (1, 0, 1, 0) more times. 11 (12, 13, 14, 15) sts.

Work even in Alternating Stripe patt until armhole measures 6$^1/_2$ (7, 7$^1/_2$, 8, 8$^1/_2$)"/16.5 (18, 19, 20.5, 21.5) cm, ending with a WS row.

Fasten off.

Right Front

Rejoin yarn to right front sts at armhole edge, starting with last dc before hdc.

Row 1 (WS): Ch1, sc in each st to end. 28 (31, 34, 37, 40) sts.

Shape Armhole and Front Neck

Row 2 (RS): Sl st in first 4 (5, 6, 7, 8) sts, ch3, dc2tog, dc to last 2 sts, dc2tog. 22 (24, 26, 28, 30) sts.

Row 3: Ch1, sc in each st to end.

Row 4 (Dec row): Ch3, dc2tog, dc to last 2 sts, dc2tog. 2 sts dec.

Rep Dec row every RS row 3 (4, 5, 5, 6) more times. 14 (14, 14, 16, 16) sts.

Next row (Neck Edge Dec row) (RS): Ch3, dc2tog, dc in each st to end. 1 st dec.

Rep Neck Edge Dec row every RS row 2 (1, 0, 1, 0) more times. 11 (12, 13, 14, 15) sts.

Work even in Alternating Stripe patt until armhole measures 6$^1/_2$ (7, 7$^1/_2$, 8, 8$^1/_2$)"/16.5 (18, 19, 20.5, 21.5) cm, ending with a WS row.

Fasten off.

Back

Rejoin yarn to back sts at left armhole edge, starting with last dc before hdc.

Row 1 (WS): Ch1, sc in each dc. 57 (63, 69, 75, 81) sts.

Row 2 (Dec row) (RS): Ch3, dc2tog, dc to last 2 sts, dc2tog. 2 sts dec.

Rep Dec row every RS row 4 (5, 6, 6, 7) more times. 47 (51, 55, 61, 65) sts.

Work even until armhole measures 6 (6$^1/_2$, 7, 7$^1/_2$, 8)"/15 (16.5, 18, 19, 20.5) cm, ending with a WS row.

Next row (RS): Ch3, dc 10 (11, 12, 13, 14), dc2tog, turn work.

Next row (WS): Ch1, sc in each st to end.

Fasten off.

Sk 23 (25, 27, 31, 33) sts at center neck and rejoin yarn for left back shoulder.

Next row (RS): Ch3, dc in each st to last 2 sts, dc2tog. 11 (12, 13, 14, 15) sts.

Next row (WS): Ch1, sc in each st to end.

Fasten off.

Finishing

Sew shoulder seams.

Armhole Edging

Join yarn at side seam. Work 1 rnd sc around armhole edge. Fasten off.

Front and Neck Edging

Join yarn at lower right front corner.

Row 1 (RS): Sc up right front edge to beginning of neck shaping, sc3 in corner, sc around neck edge to left front neck corner, sc3 in corner, sc down left front edge to lower corner, turn work.

Row 2 (Buttonhole row) (WS): Sc in each sc to left neck corner, sc3 in corner st, sc around left neck edge, sc2tog at beginning of back neck, sc in each sc to end of back neck, sc2tog, sc around right neck edge to corner, sc3 in corner st, sc in next st, *ch2, sk2, sc in next 6 sts; rep from * 7 more times, ch2, sk2, sc in each st to end.

Row 3: Sc in each sc and sc 2 in each ch-2 sp to corner, sc3 in corner st, sc around neck edge to left neck corner, sc3 in corner st, sc in each sc to end.

Row 4: Sc in each sc to left neck corner, sc3 in corner st, sc around left neck edge, sc2tog at beginning of back neck, sc in each sc to end of back neck, sc2tog, sc around right neck edge to corner, sc3 in corner st, sc in each sc to end.

Fasten off.

Sew buttons to left front to correspond with buttonholes. Weave in ends. Block lightly.

Pacheco

The deep ruffle around the V-neck brings romance to this tank. Choose a yarn with lots of drape so the ruffle flows gracefully.

SKILL LEVEL
Intermediate

SIZES
Women's Extra Small (Small, Medium, Large, Extra Large)

FINISHED MEASUREMENTS
Bust: 32 (36, 40, 44, 48)"/81.5 (91.5, 101.5, 112, 122) cm

YARN
LB Collection Cotton Bamboo, light weight #3 yarn
   (52% cotton, 48% rayon from bamboo; 245 yd./3.5 oz.,
   224 m/100 g per skein)
• 4 (4, 5, 5, 6) skeins #135 Persimmon

HOOKS & NOTIONS
• US size H-8/5 mm crochet hook
• US size I-9/5.5 mm crochet hook
• Tapestry needle

GAUGE
16 sts and 14 rows in Hi-Lo patt = 4"/10 cm

PATTERN NOTES
• Turning chain is not included in stitch counts.
• See page 91 for a photo tutorial on dc2tog.

STITCH PATTERN

Hi-Lo Pattern
Row 1: Ch1, *sc in dc, dc in sc; rep from * to end.
Rep Row 1 for patt.

Back

With smaller hook, ch 65 (73, 81, 89, 97).

Set-up row (WS): Sc in 2nd ch from hook and in each ch to end. 64 (72, 80, 88, 96) sts.

Work in Hi-Lo patt until piece measures 14"/35.5 cm, ending last row 2 (4, 4, 6, 6) sts before end of row.

Shape Armholes

Next row: Ch1, work in patt to last 2 (4, 4, 6, 6) sts, turn. 60 (64, 72, 76, 84) sts.

Next row (Dec row): Ch1, dc2tog, work in patt to last 2 sts, dc2tog, turn. 2 sts dec.

Continuing in Hi-Lo patt, rep Dec row every other row 9 (11, 13, 15, 17) more times. 40 (40, 44, 44, 48) sts.

Shape Back Neck

Next row: Ch1, work 6 sts in patt, turn.

Next row: Ch1, work in patt to end.

Fasten off.

Join yarn to opposite shoulder 6 sts from end of row.

Next row: Ch1, work in patt to end.

Next row: Ch1, work in patt to end.

Fasten off.

Front

Work same as for Back until piece measures 14"/35.5 cm, ending last row 2 (4, 4, 6, 6) sts before end of row.

Mark center of piece.

Shape Left Armhole and Left Front Neck

Row 1 (RS): Ch1, dc2tog, work in patt to 2 sts before center marker, dc2tog, turn. 2 sts dec.

Row 2 (WS): Ch1, work in patt to end.

Row 3: Ch1, dc2tog, work in patt to last 2 sts, dc2tog. 2 sts dec.

Row 4: Ch1, work in patt to end.

Rep [Rows 3–4] 8 (10, 12, 14, 16) times.

Sizes Extra Small, Small and Medium ONLY

Next row (RS): Ch1, work in patt to 2 sts before end, dc2tog, turn. 1 st dec.

Next row (WS): Ch1, work in patt to end.

Rep last 2 rows 3 (1, 1) more time(s).

All Sizes

6 sts rem.
Fasten off.

Shape Right Armhole and Right Front Neck

With RS facing, rejoin yarn at center marker.
Row 1 (RS): Ch1, dc2tog, work in patt to last 4 (6, 6, 8, 8) sts, dc2tog, turn. 2 sts dec.
Row 2 (WS): Ch1, work in patt to end.
Row 3: Ch1, dc2tog, work in patt to last 2 sts, dc2tog. 2 sts dec.
Row 4: Ch1, work in patt to end.
Rep [Rows 3–4] 8 (10, 12, 14, 16) times.

Sizes Extra Small, Small, and Medium ONLY

Next row (RS): Ch1, dc2tog, work in patt to end. 1 st dec.
Next row (WS): Ch1, work in patt to end.
Rep last 2 rows 3 (1, 1) more time(s).

All Sizes

6 sts rem.
Fasten off.

Finishing

Sew shoulder seams. Sew side seams.

Armhole Edging

Join yarn at side seam. With smaller hook, work 1 rnd sc around armhole edge.
Fasten off.

Collar

Join yarn at shoulder seam.
Rnd 1: With smaller hook, work 1 rnd sc around neck edge. Join with sl st to first st. Precise st count is not important, but it should be an even number of sts.
Change to larger hook.
Rnd 2: Ch3, *dc in next st, dc2 in next st; rep from * to end, join with sl st in 3rd ch of beginning ch-3.
Rnd 3: Ch3, *dc in next st, dc2 in next st; rep from * to end, join with sl st in 3rd ch of beginning ch-3.
Rnds 4–6: Ch3, dc in each st to end, join with sl st in 3rd ch of beginning ch-3.
Fasten off.
Weave in ends. Block lightly.

Octavia

I s edgy crochet an oxymoron? Not with this linen tank. The simple high-front neckline gives no hints about the surprise in the back—an open wrap joined at the shoulders.

SKILL LEVEL
Intermediate

SIZES
Women's Extra Small (Small, Medium, Large, Extra Large)

FINISHED MEASUREMENTS
Bust: $30^1/_2$ ($34^1/_4$, 38, 42, $45^3/_4$)"/77.5 (87, 96.5, 106.5, 116) cm

YARN
Quince & Co. Sparrow, fine weight #2 yarn (100% organic linen; 168 yd./1.75 oz., 155 m/50 g per skein)
- 4 (5, 6, 6, 7) skeins #205 Little Fern

HOOKS & NOTIONS
- US size F-5/3.75 mm crochet hook
- Tapestry needle

GAUGE
21 sts and 13 rows in Alternating Rows patt = 4"/10 cm

PATTERN NOTES
- Octavia is worked in one piece from the bottom up. The only seams are at the shoulders.
- See page 91 for a photo tutorial on dc2tog.

STITCH PATTERN

Alternating Rows Pattern
Row 1 (RS): Ch3, sk first sc, dc in each sc to end, ending with dc in beginning ch-1.
Row 2 (WS): Ch1, sk first dc, sc in each dc to end, ending with sc in 3rd ch of beginning ch-3.
Rep Rows 1–2 for patt.

Body

Ch 147 (167, 187, 207, 227).

Row 1 (RS): Sc in 2nd ch from hook and in each ch to end, turn. 146 (166, 186, 206, 226) sc.

Row 2 (WS): Ch3, dc2 in first sc, dc in each sc to last 2 sc, dc2 in next sc, dc in next sc, turn. 2 sts inc.

Row 3: Ch1, sc in each dc to end, turn.

Rep [Rows 2–3] 21 (21, 22, 22, 23) more times. 190 (210, 232, 252, 274) sts.

Left Back

Row 1 (RS): Ch3, dc2 in first sc, dc in next 42 (46, 52, 55, 60) sc, dc2tog, hdc, sc, sl st, turn.

Row 2 (WS): Ch1, sl st in first 4 sts, ch1, sc in each dc to end.

Row 3: Ch3, dc2 in first sc, dc in each sc to last 5 sc, dc2tog, hdc, sc, sl st, turn.

Row 4: Ch1, sl st in first 4 sts, ch1, sc in each dc to end.

Rep [Rows 3–4] 8 (9, 10, 11, 12) more times. 8 (8, 10, 9, 10) sts rem.

Work 4 (2, 0, 0, 0) rows even in Alternating Rows patt. Fasten off.

Front

With RS facing, sk 14 (16, 16, 20, 22) sts for armhole and rejoin yarn.

Row 1 (RS): Ch3, dc2tog, dc in next 60 (68, 78, 84, 92) sc, dc2tog, dc, turn.

Row 2 (WS): Ch1, sc2tog, sc in each dc to last 3 dc, sc2tog, sc, turn.

Row 3: Ch3, dc2tog, dc in each sc to last 3 sc, dc2tog, dc, turn.

Rep [Rows 2–3] 2 (4, 5, 5, 6) more times. 52 (52, 58, 64, 68) sts.

Work 13 (9, 7, 9, 9) rows even in Alternating Rows patt.

Shape Front Neck

Row 1 (RS): Ch3, dc 7 (7, 9, 8, 9), dc2tog, dc, turn.
Row 2 (WS): Ch1, sc2tog, sc in each dc to end. 8 (8, 10, 9, 10) sts rem.
Work 2 rows even in Alternating Rows patt.
Fasten off.
Sk 32 (32, 34, 42, 44) sts for center front neck and rejoin yarn.
Row 1 (RS): Ch3, dc2tog, dc in each sc to end, turn.
Row 2 (WS): Ch1, sc in each dc to last 3 sc, sc2tog, sc. 8 (8, 10, 9, 10) sts rem.
Work 2 rows even in Alternating Rows patt.
Fasten off.

Right Back

With RS facing, sk 14 (16, 16, 20, 22) sts for armhole and rejoin yarn.
Row 1 (RS): Ch1, sl st, hdc, dc2tog, dc in each sc to last 2 sc, dc2 in next st, dc in last dc, turn.
Row 2 (WS): Ch1, sc in each st to last dc, sl st in top of dc2tog, turn.
Rep [Rows 1–2] 9 (10, 11, 12, 13) more times. 8 (8, 10, 9, 10) sts rem.
Work 4 (2, 0, 0, 0) rows even in Alternating Rows patt.
Fasten off.

Finishing

Sew shoulder seams, crossing right back over left back.

Edging

Join yarn at any shoulder seam. Work 1 rnd sc around edge. Surprisingly, there is only one edge on this piece, which winds around the armholes, neck, and lower edge.
Weave in ends. Block.

Woodside

The beaded fringe on this flirty tank just might inspire you to dance! Beads also outline the neck and armholes. I used matte copper-colored beads for a subtle accent against the denim yarn.

SKILL LEVEL
Easy

SIZES
Women's Extra Small (Small, Medium, Large, Extra Large)

FINISHED MEASUREMENTS
Bust: 34$^1/_2$ (38$^1/_2$, 42$^1/_4$, 46, 50)"/88 (97.5, 107.5, 117, 127) cm

YARN
Kollage Yarns Riveting Sport, light weight #3 yarn (95% cotton, 5% other; 350 yd./3.5 oz., 320 m/100 g per skein)
- 3 (3, 3, 4, 4) skeins #7902 Dusk Denim

HOOKS & NOTIONS
- US size G-6/4 mm crochet hook
- 1.4 oz./40 g size 6/0 glass beads
- Tapestry needle
- Large-eye beading needle

GAUGE
25 sts and 9 rows in Double Cluster patt = 4"/10 cm

PATTERN NOTES
- Turning chain counts as a stitch throughout.
- See pages 91–93 for photo tutorials on dc2tog and sc with beads.

STITCH PATTERN

Double Cluster
Row 1: Ch3, dc in first dc2tog, dc2tog in each dc2tog to end of row.
Rep Row 1 for patt.

Back

Ch 111 (123, 135, 147, 159).

Set-up row (RS): Dc in 4th ch from hook, *dc2tog over next 2 ch; rep from * to end. 108 (120, 132, 144, 156) sts.

Begin working Double Cluster patt. Work even until piece measures 13 (13, 13^1/$_2$, 13^1/$_2$, 14)"/33 (33, 34.5, 34.5, 35.5) cm, ending with a WS row.

Shape Armholes

Next row (RS): Sl st 2 in first 4 (5, 6, 6, 7) dc2tog, sl st in next dc2tog, ch3, dc in same dc2tog, dc2tog in each dc2tog to last 4 (5, 6, 6, 7) dc2tog, turn.

Next row (Dec row): Ch2, dc in first dc2tog, dc2tog over next 2 dc2tog, dc2tog in each dc2tog to last 3 dc2tog, dc2tog over next 2 dc2tog, dc2tog in last dc2tog, turn. 4 sts dec.

Rep Dec row every row 6 (7, 9, 11, 12) more times. 72 (78, 80, 84, 90) sts.

Work 2 (1, 1, 1, 0) row(s) even in patt.

Right Back Neck

Row 1 (RS): Ch3, dc in first dc2tog, dc2tog in each of next 6 (7, 7, 8, 9) dc2tog, dc2tog over next 2 dc2tog, dc2tog in next dc2tog, turn.

Row 2 (WS): Ch3, dc in first dc2tog, dc2tog over next 2 dc2tog, dc2tog in each dc2tog to end.

(continued)

Row 3: Ch3, dc in first dc2tog, dc2tog in each dc2tog to last 3 dc2tog, dc2tog over next 2 dc2tog, dc2tog in next dc2tog, turn.

Row 4: Rep Row 2. 12 (14, 14, 16, 18) sts.

Work 2 rows even.

Fasten off.

Left Back Neck

Skipping center 16 (17, 18, 18, 19) dc2tog, rejoin yarn with RS facing.

Row 1 (RS): Ch3, dc in first dc2tog, dc2tog over next 2 dc2tog, dc2tog in each dc2tog to end.

Row 2 (WS): Ch3, dc in first dc2tog, dc2tog in each dc2tog to last 3 dc2tog, dc2tog over next 2 dc2tog, dc2tog in next dc2tog.

Rows 3–4: Rep Rows 1–2. 12 (14, 14, 16, 18) sts.

Work 2 rows even.

Fasten off.

Front

Work same as back until fourth row of armhole shaping is complete. Continue armhole shaping while shaping front neck.

Left Front Neck

Mark center of row just completed.

Row 1 (RS): Continuing armhole shaping, work to 3 dc2tog before marked center, dc2tog over next 2 dc2tog, dc2tog in next dc2tog, turn.

Row 2 (WS): Ch3, dc in first dc2tog, dc2tog over next 2 dc2tog, work in patt to end continuing armhole shaping if necessary.

Row 3: Continuing armhole shaping if necessary, work to last 3 dc2tog, dc2tog over next 2 dc2tog, dc2tog in next dc2tog.

Rep Rows 2–3 until 12 (14, 14, 16, 18) sts rem.

Work even if needed until same length as back.

Fasten off.

Right Front Neck

Join yarn at marked center.

Row 1 (RS): Ch 3, dc in first dc2tog, dc2tog over next 2 dc2tog, work in patt to end, continuing armhole shaping if necessary.

Row 2 (WS): Continuing armhole shaping if necessary, work to last 3 dc2tog, dc2tog over next 2 dc2tog, dc2tog in next dc2tog.

Rep Rows 1–2 until 12 (14, 14, 16, 18) sts rem.

Work even if needed until same length as back.

Fasten off.

Finishing

Sew shoulder seams. Sew side seams.

Using a second ball of yarn and large-eye beading needle, string about 220 (250, 280, 310, 340) beads onto yarn.

Neck Edging

Join yarn at a shoulder seam.

Rnd 1 (RS): Using unbeaded yarn, work 1 rnd sc around neck edge, join to first st of rnd with sl st. Turn work.

Rnd 2 (WS): Change to beaded yarn. Ch 1, sc in first st, *slide 1 bead up against st just made, sc in next 2 sts; rep from * to end, join to first st of rnd with sl st.

Fasten off.

Armhole Edging

Join yarn at side seam.

Rnd 1 (RS): Using unbeaded yarn, work 1 rnd sc around armhole edge, join to first st of rnd with sl st. Turn work.

Rnd 2 (WS): Change to beaded yarn. Ch 1, sc in first st, *slide 1 bead up against st just made, sc in next 2 sts; rep from * to end, join to first st of rnd with sl st.

Fasten off.

Rep for other armhole.

Hem Edging

Join yarn at a side seam.

Rnd 1 (RS): Using unbeaded yarn, work 1 rnd sc around lower edge, join to first st of rnd with sl st. Turn work.

Rnd 2 (WS): Change to beaded yarn. Ch 1, sc in first st, *slide 1 bead up against st just made, sc in next 2 sts; rep from * to end, join to first st of rnd with sl st.

Fasten off.

Weave in ends. Block.

Fringe

Count beads around lower edge.

Measure and cut the same number of 8"/20.5 cm strands of yarn as you counted beads.

For each strand: Tie an overhand knot near one end of the strand of yarn. Using large-eye beading needle, thread 2 beads on the strand. Tie an overhand knot near the other end of the strand. Slide a bead down toward each end until it stops at the knot.

Insert crochet hook through the lower edge of tank from RS to WS in the space between 2 beads. Use hook to pull center of beaded strand though, making a loop. Pull beaded ends of strand through this loop and pull tight.

Repeat in each space between beads around entire lower edge.

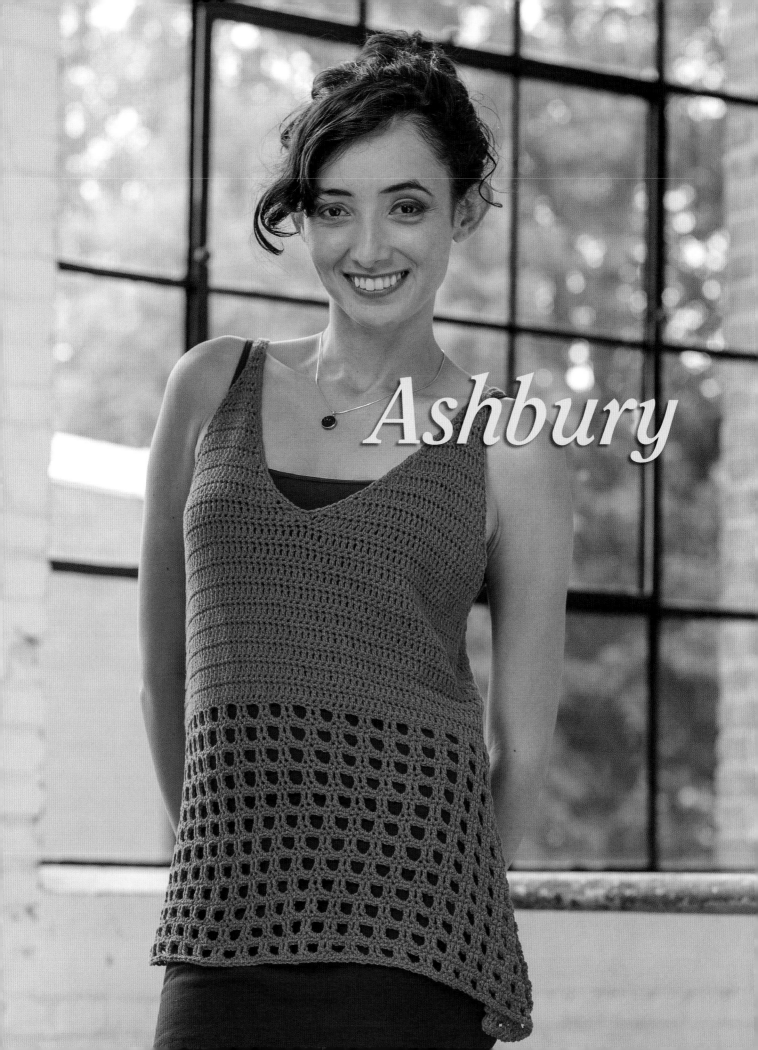

Ashbury

This playful camisole has a deep V-neck on one side and a scoop on the other—you decide which is the front. The openwork skirt drops to an asymmetrical point on one side.

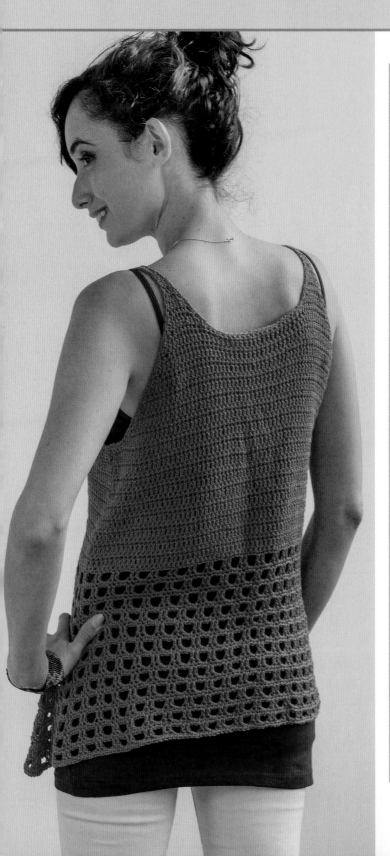

SKILL LEVEL
Intermediate

SIZES
Women's Small (Medium, Large, Extra Large, 2X Large)

FINISHED MEASUREMENTS
Bust: 34³/₄ (38¹/₂, 42¹/₄, 46, 50)"/88.5 (98, 107.5, 117, 127) cm

YARN
Universal Yarns Bamboo Pop, light weight #3 yarn
   (50% cotton, 50% bamboo; 292 yd./3.5 oz., 266 m/
   100 g per skein)
- 3 (3, 3, 3, 4) skeins #114 Super Pink

HOOKS & NOTIONS
- US size H-8/5 mm crochet hook
- Tapestry needle

GAUGE
17 sts and 13 rows in Alternating Rows Patt = 4"/10 cm

PATTERN NOTES
- Turning chain is included in stitch counts throughout.
- See pages 86 and 91 for photo tutorials of sc2tog and dc2tog.

STITCH PATTERN

Alternating Rows Pattern
Row 1 (RS): Ch3, sk first sc, dc in each sc to end, ending with
   dc in beginning ch-1.
Row 2 (WS): Ch1, sk first dc, sc in each dc to end, ending
   with sc in 3rd ch of beginning ch-3.
Rep Rows 1–2 for patt.

Back

Ch 75 (83, 91, 99, 107).
Set-up row (WS): Sc in 2nd ch from hook and in each ch to
   end. 74 (82, 90, 98, 106) sts.
Work in Alternating Rows patt until piece measures 5"/12.5
   cm, ending with a WS row and ending last row 4 (5, 6, 7,
   8) sts before end of row.

Shape Armholes

Row 1 (RS): Ch3, sk first sc, dc in each sc to last 4 (5, 6, 7, 8) sc, turn. 66 (72, 78, 84, 90) sts.

Row 2 (WS): Ch1, sk first dc, sc2tog over next 2 dc, sc in each dc to last 2 dc, sc2tog, turn. 2 sts dec.

Row 3: Ch3, sk first sc, dc2tog over next 2 sc, dc in each sc to last 2 sc, dc2tog, turn. 2 sts dec.

Rep [Rows 2–3] 5 (6, 7, 8, 9) more times. 42 (44, 46, 48, 50) sts.

Shape Back Neck

Row 1 (WS): Ch1, sk first dc, sc2tog over next 2 dc, sc in next 6 dc, sc2tog, turn.

Row 2 (RS): Ch3, sk first sc, dc2tog over next 2 sc, dc in each sc to last 2 sc, dc2tog, turn.

Row 3: Ch1, sk first dc, sc2tog over next 2 dc, sc in each dc to last 2 dc, sc2tog, turn.

Row 4: Ch3, sk first sc, dc2tog twice, turn.

Row 5: Ch1, sc2tog. Break yarn and fasten off.

With WS facing, sk 22 (24, 26, 28, 30) dc and rejoin yarn.

Row 1 (WS): Ch1, sk first dc, sc2tog over next 2 dc, sc in each dc to last 2 dc, sc2tog, turn.

Row 2 (RS): Ch3, sk first sc, dc2tog over next 2 sc, dc in each sc to last 2 sc, dc2tog, turn.

Row 3: Ch1, sk first dc, sc2tog over next 2 dc, sc in each dc to last 2 dc, sc2tog, turn.

Row 4: Ch3, sk first sc, dc2tog twice, turn.

Row 5: Ch1, sc2tog. Break yarn and fasten off.

Front

Work same as for back to beginning of armhole shaping. Mark center of piece.

Shape Left Front Armhole and Neck

Row 1 (RS): Ch3, sk first sc, dc in each sc to center marker, turn. 33 (36, 39, 42, 45) sts.

Row 2 (WS): Ch1, sk first dc, sc2tog over next 2 dc, sc in each dc to last 2 dc, sc2tog, turn. 2 sts dec.

Row 3: Ch3, sk first sc, dc2tog over next 2 sc, dc in each sc to last 2 sc, dc2tog, turn. 2 sts dec.

Rep [Rows 2–3] 6 (7, 8, 9, 9) more times. 5 (4, 3, 2, 5) sts rem.

Sizes Small, Medium and 2X Large Only

Next row (WS): Ch1, sk first dc, sc2tog over next 2 dc, sc in each dc to last 2 dc, sc2tog, turn. 3 (2, 3, 2, 3) sts rem.

Break yarn and fasten off.

Shape Right Front Armhole and Neck

With RS facing, rejoin yarn at center marker. Work same as left front armhole and neck. Sew side seams.

Skirt

Join yarn to lower edge at right side seam.

Rnd 1: Ch1, sc 74 (82, 90, 98, 106) across front to left side seam, pm, sc 74 (82, 90, 98, 106) across back, join with sl st to beginning ch-1. 148 (164, 180, 196, 212) sc.

Rnd 2: Ch3 (counts as dc), sk first sc, dc in next sc, *ch2, sk2, dc in next 2 sc; rep from * to last 2 sc, ch2, join with sl st to 3rd ch of beginning ch-3.

Rnd 3: Ch1 (counts as sc), sc in dc, *sc2 in ch-2 sp, sc in next 2 dc; rep from * to last ch-2 sp, sc2 in ch-2 sp, join with sl st to beginning ch-1.

Rnd 4: Ch3 (counts as dc), sk first sc, dc in next sc, *ch2, sk2, dc in next 2 sc; rep from * to scs in ch-2 sp just before marker at left side seam, ch2, dc2 in marked ch-2 sp, **ch2, dc in next 2 dc; rep from ** to last 2 sc, ch2, join with sl st to 3rd ch of beginning ch-3.

Rnd 5: Ch1 (counts as sc), sc in dc, *sc2 in ch-2 sp, sc in next 2 dc; rep from * to last ch-2 sp, sc2 in ch-2 sp, join with sl st to beginning ch-1.

Rnd 6: Ch3 (counts as dc), sk first sc, dc in next sc, *ch2, sk2, dc in next 2 sc; rep from * to dcs worked in ch-2 sp at left side seam, ch2, dc2 in next dc, ch2, dc in next dc, **ch2, dc in next 2 dc; rep from ** to last 2 sc, ch2, join with sl st to 3rd ch of beginning ch-3.

Rnds 7–22: Rep Rnds 3–6 four more times.

Rnd 23: Rep Rnd 3.

Rnd 24: Rep Rnd 4.

Rnd 25: Rep Rnd 5.

Fasten off.

Finishing

Join yarn to point at top of left front. Ch10 and join with sl st to point at top of left back. Rep on right front.

Neck Edging

Join yarn at back neck. Work 1 rnd sc around neck edge, working into back bumps of ch at shoulders. Fasten off.

Armhole Edging

Join yarn at side seam. Work 1 rnd sc around armhole edge, working into other side of ch at shoulders. Fasten off. Weave in ends. Block lightly.

Divisidero

The curved hem and A-line shape of this tank let you cover your behind without being all covered up. The beautiful linen yarn and deep scoop neck keep it cool.

SKILL LEVEL
Easy

SIZES
Women's Extra Small (Small, Medium, Large, Extra Large, 2X Large)

FINISHED MEASUREMENTS
Bust: 32 (35^3/$_4$, 39^1/$_2$, 43, 46^3/$_4$, 50^1/$_2$)"/81.5 (91, 100.5, 109, 118.5, 128.5) cm

YARN
Quince & Co. Kestrel, medium weight #4 yarn (100% organic linen; 76 yd./1.75 oz., 70 m/50 g per skein)
- 6 (7, 7, 8, 9, 10) skeins #502 Porpoise

HOOKS & NOTIONS
- US size J-10/6 mm crochet hook
- Tapestry needle

GAUGE
13 sts and 10 rows in hdc = 4"/10 cm

PATTERN NOTES
- Divisidero is worked in one piece. The curved lower edge is shaped with short rows.
- While it is worked in the round, the work is turned at the end of each round, so you will work both RS and WS rounds.
- Turning ch counts as hdc throughout.
- See pages 87–89 for photo tutorials on hdc and hdc2tog.

Back

Ch 130 (142, 154, 166, 178, 190).

Rnd 1 (RS): Hdc in 3rd ch from hook and in each ch to end, join with sl st in top of ch, turn. 128 (140, 152, 164, 176, 188) hdc.

Rnd 2 (WS): Ch2 (counts as hdc), hdc in each st to end, join with sl st in beginning ch-2, turn.

Short row 1 (RS): Ch2, hdc 24 (30, 36, 42, 48, 54), turn.

Short row 2 (WS): Ch2, hdc in each hdc, hdc2tog over beginning ch-2 of prior row and next st in Rnd 2 below, hdc in next 6 hdc, turn.

Short row 3: Ch2, hdc in each hdc, hdc2tog over beginning ch-2 of prior row and next st in Rnd 2 below, hdc in next 6 hdc turn.

Short rows 4–13: Rep Short Rows 2 and 3 five more times.

Short row 14 (WS): Ch2, hdc in each hdc, hdc2tog over beginning ch-2 of prior row and next st of Rnd 2 below, hdc in next 6 hdc, turn.

Rnd 3 (RS): Ch2, hdc in each hdc, hdc2tog over beginning ch-2 of prior row and next st of Rnd 2 below, hdc to end of rnd, join with sl st in beginning ch-2. 114 (126, 138, 150, 162, 174) hdc. Break yarn.

Sk next 16 sts and rejoin yarn with WS facing. This is right "side seam."

Rnd 4: Ch2, hdc in each hdc, join with sl st in beginning ch-2, turn.

Rnds 5–6: Rep Rnd 4 twice.

Rnd 7: Ch2, hdc 3, hdc2tog over next 2 hdc, hdc 47 (53, 59, 65, 71, 77), hdc2tog over next 2 hdc, hdc6, hdc2tog over next 2 hdc, hdc to last 5 hdc, hdc2tog over next 2 hdc, hdc3, join with sl st in beginning ch-2, turn. 110 (122, 134, 146, 158, 170) hdc.

Rnds 8–12: Rep Rnd 4 five times.

Rnd 13: Ch2, hdc 3, hdc2tog over next 2 hdc, hdc 45 (51, 57, 63, 69, 75), hdc2tog over next 2 hdc, hdc6, hdc2tog over next 2 hdc, hdc to last 5 hdc, hdc2tog over next 2 hdc, hdc3, join with sl st in beginning ch-2, turn. 106 (118, 130, 142, 154, 166) hdc.

Rnds 14–18: Rep Rnd 4 five times.

Rnd 19: Ch2, hdc2tog over first 2 hdc, hdc 51 (57, 63, 69, 75, 81), hdc2tog over next 2 hdc, hdc to end, join with sl st in beginning ch-2, turn. 104 (116, 128, 140, 152, 164) hdc.

Rep [Rnd 4] 1 (1, 3, 3, 5, 5) more times. Fasten off.

Shape Armholes

With RS facing, counting from end of rnd, sk 3 (4, 5, 6, 7, 8) hdc and join yarn.

Row 1 (RS): Ch2, hdc 46 (50, 54, 58, 62, 66), turn.

Row 2 (WS): Ch2, hdc2tog, hdc to last hdc, hdc2tog, hdc in top of beginning ch-2, turn. 2 sts dec.

Rep [Row 2] 4 (5, 6, 8, 9, 10) more times. 36 (38, 40, 40, 42, 44) hdc.

Work 8 (7, 8, 6, 7, 6) rows even in hdc.

Shape Back Neck

Row 1 (RS): Ch2, hdc 6, hdc2tog, turn.
Row 2 (WS): Ch2, hdc2tog, hdc to end, turn.
Work 4 rows even in hdc. Fasten off.
With RS facing, sk 20 (22, 24, 24, 26, 28) hdc and rejoin yarn.
Next row (RS): Ch2, hdc2tog, hdc to end, turn.
Next row (WS): Ch2, hdc 5, hdctog, turn.
Work 4 rows even in hdc. Fasten off.

Front

With RS facing, sk 6 (8, 10, 12, 14, 16) sts for armhole and join yarn.

Row 1 (RS): Ch2, hdc 46 (50, 54, 58, 62, 66), turn.

Row 2 (WS): Ch2, hdc2tog, hdc to last hdc, hdc2tog, hdc in top of beginning ch-2, turn. 2 sts dec.

Rep [Row 2] 2 more times. 40 (44, 48, 52, 56, 60) hdc.

Shape Front Neck

Row 1 (RS): Ch2, hdc2tog, hdc 6 (7, 8, 10, 11, 12), hdc2tog, turn.

Row 2 (WS): Ch2, hdc2tog, hdc to last 2 hdc, hdc2tog, turn.

Continue dec at armhole edge only every row 0 (1, 2, 4, 5, 6) more time(s). 8 sts rem.

Work 14 (13, 14, 12, 13, 12) rows even in hdc. Fasten off.

With RS facing, sk 20 (22, 24, 24, 26, 28) hdc at center front neck and join yarn.

Next row (RS): Ch2, hdc2tog, hdc to last 2 hdc, hdc2tog, turn.

Next row (WS): Ch2, hdc2tog, hdc to last 2 hdc, hdc2tog, turn.

Continue dec at armhole edge only every row 0 (1, 2, 4, 5, 6) more time(s). 8 sts rem.

Work 14 (13, 14, 12, 13, 12) rows even in hdc. Fasten off.

Finishing

Sew shoulder seams.

Neck Edging

Join yarn at right shoulder seam. Work 1 rnd sc around neck edge.

Armhole Edging

Join yarn at side seam. Work 1 rnd sc around armhole edge.

Weave in ends. Block lightly.

Marina

The crisp linen yarn in this tunic brings the ornate stitchwork into bold relief. The simple shape and rich color make this piece a modern classic.

SKILL LEVEL
Intermediate

SIZES
Women's Extra Small (Small, Medium, Large, Extra Large)

FINISHED MEASUREMENTS
Bust: 36¼ (39, 41¾, 44½, 47¼)"/92 (99, 106, 113, 120) cm

YARN
Louet Euroflax Sport, fine weight #2 yarn (100% wet spun linen; 270 yd./3.5 oz., 246 m/100 g per skein)
- 3 (4, 4, 4, 5) skeins #18-2464 Cedarwood

HOOKS & NOTIONS
- US size F-5/3.75 mm crochet hook
- Tapestry needle

GAUGE
23 sts and 8 rows in Shell Stripe patt = 4"/10 cm

STITCH PATTERN

Shell Stripe Pattern
Set-up row: Ch4 (counts as dc, ch1), *sk first dc, dc in next dc, ch1; rep to last st, dc in 3rd ch of turning ch.
Row 1: Ch3 (counts as dc), *sk next 2 ch-1 sps, (3dc, ch2, 3dc) in next dc, sk next 2 ch-1 sps, dc in next dc; rep from * to end, ending with last dc in 3rd ch of beginning ch-4.
Row 2: Ch6 (counts as dc, ch3), *sc in next ch-2 sp, ch3, sk next 3 dc, dc in next dc, ch3; rep from * to end, ending last rep with dc in 3rd ch of beginning ch-3.
Row 3: Ch4 (counts as dc, ch1), *dc in next ch-3 loop, ch1, dc in next sc, ch1, dc in next ch-3 loop, ch1, dc in next dc, ch1; rep from * to end, ending last rep with dc in 3rd ch of beginning ch-6.
Row 4: Ch3 (counts as dc), sk first dc, dc in each dc and ch-1 sp to end, ending with dc in 3rd ch of beginning ch-4.
Row 5: Ch4 (counts as dc, ch1), sk first 2 dc, dc in next dc, *ch1, sk next dc, dc in next dc; rep from * to end, ending with last dc in 3rd ch of beginning ch-3.
Rep Rows 1–5 for patt.

Work even until armhole measures 9$\frac{1}{2}$ (10, 10$\frac{1}{2}$, 11, 11$\frac{1}{2}$)"/24 (25.5, 26.5, 28, 29) cm.
Fasten off.

Front

Work same as back until 5 rows of armhole shaping have been worked, ending with a WS row. *NOTE: Front neck shaping begins before armhole shaping is complete.*

Shape Left Front Neck

Mark center 40 (40, 40, 48, 48) sts.
Row 1 (RS): Continuing armhole shaping, work to 4 sts past first neck marker, turn.
Row 2 (WS): Ch1, sl st 2, work in patt to end.
Row 3: Work in patt to last 2 sts, turn.
Armhole and neck shaping are complete. 12 (16, 16, 16, 16) sts remain.
Work in patt until same length as back to shoulder.
Fasten off.

Shape Right Front Neck

With RS facing, rejoin yarn 4 sts before second neck marker.
Row 1 (RS): Ch3, work in patt to end, continuing armhole shaping.
Row 2 (WS): Work in patt to last 2 sts, turn.
Row 3: Ch1, sl st 2, work in patt to end.
Armhole and neck shaping are complete. 12 (16, 16, 16, 16) sts remain.
Work in patt until same length as back to shoulder.
Fasten off.

Finishing

Sew side seams. Sew shoulder seams.

Neck Edging

Join yarn at right shoulder seam. Work 1 rnd sc around neck edge. Fasten off.

Armhole Edging

Join yarn at side seam. Work 1 rnd sc around armhole edge. Fasten off.
Weave in ends. Block.

Back

Ch 107 (115, 123, 131, 139).
Foundation row (WS): Dc in 3rd ch from hook, dc in each ch to end. 104 (112, 120, 128, 136) dc.
Begin working Shell Stripe patt.
Work even in patt until piece measures 17$\frac{1}{2}$ (18, 18$\frac{1}{2}$, 19, 19$\frac{1}{2}$)"/44.5 (45.5, 47, 48.5, 49.5) cm, ending with a RS row.

Shape Armholes

Row 1 (WS): Ch1, sl st in 8 (8, 10, 10, 12) sts, work in patt to last 8 (8, 10, 10, 12) sts, turn.
Row 2 (RS): Ch 1, sl st 2, work in patt to last 2 sts, turn.
Rep Row 2, decreasing 2 sts at each end of every row 5 (5, 6, 6, 7) more times. 64 (72, 72, 80, 80) sts.

Bernal

The close stitchwork on the buttoned bodice of this tank gives you coverage where you want it, while the delicate shell mesh pattern in the skirt keeps it airy. The hand-dyed linen is crisp enough that the openwork skirt won't go limp.

SKILL LEVEL
Intermediate

SIZES
Women's Small (Medium, Large, Extra Large, 2X Large)

FINISHED MEASUREMENTS
Bust: 33$\frac{1}{4}$ (37$\frac{1}{4}$, 41$\frac{1}{4}$, 45$\frac{1}{4}$, 49$\frac{1}{4}$)"/84.5 (94.5, 105, 115, 125) cm

YARN
Fiesta Yarns Linnette, fine weight #2 yarn (70% linen, 30% Pima cotton; 380 yd./3.5 oz., 347 m/100 g per skein)
- 2 (3, 3, 3, 3) skeins #110 Caribbean

HOOKS & NOTIONS
- US size F-5/3.75 mm crochet hook
- Tapestry needle
- 4 buttons, $\frac{5}{8}$"/15 mm diameter

GAUGE
20 sts and 14 rows in hdc = 4"/10 cm

PATTERN NOTES
- Bodice section is worked first, from waist to shoulders. The skirt section is worked down from waist.
- Turning chain counts as hdc throughout bodice section.
- See pages 87–89 for photo tutorials on hdc and hdc2tog.

STITCH PATTERN

Shell Mesh Pattern
Rnd 1: Ch5, *sk 2 sc, sc in next sc, ch4; rep from * to end, ending by joining with sl st in 2nd ch of beginning ch-5.
Rnd 2: Ch5, *sc in ch-4 sp, (dc3, ch3, dc3) in next ch-4 sp, sc in next ch-4 sp, ch4; rep from * to end, ending with ch2, sl st in 3rd ch of beginning ch-5.
Rnd 3: Ch4, sk ch-2 sp, *(sc, ch4, sc) in ch-3 sp, ch4, sc in ch-4 sp, ch4; rep from * to end, ending with ch-4, sl st in 1st ch of beginning ch-4.
Rep Rnds 2–3 for patt.

Bodice

Ch 152 (172, 192, 212, 232).

Row 1 (RS): Hdc in 3rd ch from hook and in each ch to end. 150 (170, 190, 210, 230) hdc.

Row 2 (WS): Ch2, hdc in each hdc to end.

Row 3: Ch2, hdc 18 (20, 22, 25, 27), hdc2 in next hdc, hdc 35 (41, 47, 51, 57), hdc2 in next hdc, hdc 40 (44, 48, 54, 58), hdc2 in next hdc, hdc 35 (41, 47, 51, 57), hdc2 in next hdc, hdc in each hdc to end. 154 (174, 194, 214, 234) hdc.

Rows 4–6: Ch2, hdc in each hdc to end.

Row 7: Ch2, hdc 18 (20, 22, 25, 27), hdc2 in next hdc, hdc 37 (43, 49, 53, 59), hdc2 in next hdc, hdc 40 (44, 48, 54, 58), hdc2 in next hdc, hdc 37 (43, 49, 53, 59), hdc2 in next hdc, hdc in each hdc to end. 158 (178, 198, 218, 238) hdc.

Rows 8–10: Ch2, hdc in each hdc to end.

Row 11: Ch2, hdc 18 (20, 22, 25, 27), hdc2 in next hdc, hdc 39 (45, 51, 55, 61), hdc2 in next hdc, hdc 40 (44, 48, 54, 58), hdc2 in next hdc, hdc 39 (45, 51, 55, 61), hdc2 in next hdc, hdc in each hdc to end. 162 (182, 202, 222, 242) hdc.

Rows 12–14: Ch2, hdc in each hdc to end.

Row 15: Ch2, hdc 18 (20, 22, 25, 27), hdc2 in next hdc, hdc 41 (47, 53, 57, 63), hdc2 in next hdc, hdc 40 (44, 48, 54, 58), hdc2 in next hdc, hdc 41 (47, 53, 57, 63), hdc2 in next hdc, hdc in each hdc to end. 166 (186, 206, 226, 246) hdc.

Row 16: Ch2, hdc in each hdc to end.

Rep [Row 16] 0 (2, 4, 6, 8) more times.

Shape Right Front Neck and Armhole

Row 1 (RS): Ch1, sl st in first 8 (8, 9, 10, 11) hdc, ch2, hdc2tog, hdc 21 (25, 28, 31, 34), hdc2tog, hdc in next st, turn.

Row 2 (WS): Ch2, hdc2tog, hdc to last 2 sts, hdc2tog, turn.

Rep Row 2 until 8 (12, 15, 18, 21) sts rem.

Working even at neck edge, dec by hdc2tog at armhole edge of next 0 (3, 5, 7, 9) rows. 8 (9, 10, 11, 12) hdc.

Work even until bodice measures $11^{1}/_2$ ($12^{3}/_4$, $13^{3}/_4$, $14^{3}/_4$, $15^{3}/_4$)"/29 (32.5, 35, 37.5, 40) cm.

Fasten off.

Shape Back Armholes

With RS facing, sk 16 (18, 20, 22, 24) for armhole and rejoin yarn.

Row 1 (RS): Ch2, hdc2tog, hdc 60 (68, 76, 84, 92), hdc2tog, hdc, turn.

Row 2 (WS): Ch2, hdc2tog, hdc in each hdc to end, hdc2tog, turn.

Rep last row until 50 (52, 56, 60, 66) hdc rem.

Work even until back section of bodice measures $10^{1}/_2$ ($11^{3}/_4$, $12^{3}/_4$, $13^{3}/_4$, $14^{3}/_4$)"/26.5 (30, 32.5, 35, 37.5) cm from beginning, ending with a WS row.

Shape Back Neck

Row 1 (RS): Ch2, hdc8 (9, 10, 11, 12), hdc2tog, turn.

Row 2 (WS): Ch2, hdc2tog, hdc to end.

Row 3: Ch2, hdc in each hdc to end.

Row 4: Ch2, hdc in each hdc to end.

Fasten off.

With RS facing, rejoin yarn 10 (11, 12, 13, 14) hdcs from end of row.

Next row (RS): Ch2, hdc2tog, hdc to end.

Next row (WS): Ch2, hdc 7 (8, 9, 10, 11), hdc2tog, turn.

Next row: Ch2, hdc in each hdc to end.

Next row: Ch2, hdc in each hdc to end.

Fasten off.

Shape Left Front Neck and Armhole

With RS facing, sk 16 (18, 20, 22, 24) for armhole and rejoin yarn.

Row 1 (RS): Ch2, hdc2tog, hdc 21 (25, 28, 31, 34), hdc2tog, hdc in next st, turn.

Row 2 (WS): Ch2, hdc2tog, hdc to last 2 sts, hdc2tog, turn.

Rep Row 2 until 8 (12, 15, 18, 21) sts rem.

Working even at neck edge, dec by hdc2tog at armhole edge of next 0 (3, 5, 7, 9) rows. 8 (9, 10, 11, 12) hdc.

Work even until bodice measures $11^{1}/_2$ ($12^{3}/_4$, $13^{3}/_4$, $14^{3}/_4$, $15^{3}/_4$)"/29 (32.5, 35, 37.5, 40) cm.

Fasten off.

Sew shoulder seams.

Front and Neck Edging

Join yarn at lower corner of right front bodice. Work 1 row of sc around front and neck edges, working 3 sc in corner sts. Turn work.

Next row (WS): Ch1, work 1 row of sc around front and neck edges, working 3 sc in corner sts. Turn work.

Mark position for 4 button loops evenly spaced along right front edge.

Next row (RS): Ch 1, *sc to marked button loop position, ch5, sc in same st as last sc; rep from * 3 more times, sc to top corner of right front, fasten off.

Pin fronts together, placing right front edging over left front edging.

Mark position on lower edge that corresponds with center of right armhole.

Skirt

Join yarn to lower edge at marked right armhole center.

Rnd 1: Ch1, sc 153 (171, 189, 207, 225) around lower edge of bodice, join with sl st in beginning ch-1.

Begin working Shell Mesh patt in the round.

Work in patt until skirt measures 10"/25.5 cm, ending with Rnd 3 of patt.

Last rnd: Ch3, dc2 in first ch of beginning ch-3, *sc in ch-4 sp, dc9 in next ch-4 sp, sc in next ch-4 sp, dc5 in sc; rep from * to end, ending with dc2 in base of beginning ch-3.

Fasten off.

Finishing

Armhole Edging

Join yarn at side seam. Work 1 rnd sc around armhole edge. Fasten off.

Sew buttons to left front to correspond to button loops.

Weave in ends. Block lightly.

Clement

This A-line tank glides easily over your hips. The high neck with its keyhole opening is a great place to feature a single special button.

SKILL LEVEL
Easy

SIZES
Women's Small (Medium, Large, Extra Large, 2X Large)

FINISHED MEASUREMENTS
Bust: $34^1/_2$ ($38^1/_4$, $41^3/_4$, $45^1/_2$, 49)"/87.5 (97, 106, 115.5, 124.5) cm

YARN
Crystal Palace Yarns Panda Silk, fine weight #2 yarn (52% bamboo, 43% superwash merino wool, 5% combed silk; 204 yd./1.75 oz., 188 m/50 g per skein)
- 8 (9, 10, 11, 12) skeins #3014 Pewter

HOOKS & NOTIONS
- US size G-6/4 mm crochet hook
- Tapestry needle
- 1 button, $^9/_{16}$"/14 mm diameter

GAUGE
18 sts and 10 rows in Staggered Double Crochet Pairs patt = 4"/10 cm

PATTERN NOTES
- Turning chain is not counted.
- See page 91 for photo tutorial on dc2tog.

STITCH PATTERN

Staggered Double Crochet Pairs
Row 1: Ch3, dc2tog over first and second ch sps, *ch1, dc2tog by inserting hook in same ch sp as last st, then in next ch sp; rep from *, working second leg of final dc2tog under beginning ch-3 of previous row, ch1, dc into 3rd ch of beginning ch-3.
Rep Row 1 for patt.

SPECIAL INSTRUCTIONS
To dec 1 pair at beginning of row: Ch3, sk first ch-1 sp, dc2tog over 2nd and 3rd ch sps, continue in patt.
To dec 1 pair at end of row: Work in patt to last dc2tog, omit final dc2tog, dc into 3rd ch of beginning ch-3.

Back

Ch 91 (99, 107, 115, 123).

Row 1 (RS): Sc in 2nd ch from hook, sc in each ch to end. 90 (98, 106, 114, 122) sts.

Row 2 (WS): Ch3, dc2tog over first and second sc, ch1, *dc2tog over next 2 sc, ch1; rep from * to last st, dc in beginning ch. 44 (48, 52, 56, 60) dc pairs.

Begin working Staggered Double Crochet Pairs patt.

Work even in patt until piece measures 3"/7.5 cm.

Next row (Dec row): Dec 1 pair at beginning and end of row (see Special Instructions at beginning of patt). 42 (46, 50, 54, 58) dc pairs.

Continuing in patt, rep Dec row every 8th row 2 more times. 38 (42, 46, 50, 54) dc pairs.

Work even until piece measures 13$\frac{1}{2}$ (14, 14$\frac{1}{2}$, 15, 15$\frac{1}{2}$)"/34.5 (35.5, 37, 38, 39.5) cm, ending with a WS row.

Shape Armholes

Row 1: Ch1, (sl st in dc2tog, sl st in ch-1 sp) 5 (6, 7, 8, 9) times, ch3, work in patt until 5 (6, 7, 8, 9) dc pairs remain, dc in same ch sp as last st, turn.

Continuing in patt, dec 1 pair at beginning and end of each row 3 times. 28 (30, 32, 34, 36) dc pairs.

Work even in patt until armhole measures 6 (6$\frac{1}{2}$, 7, 7$\frac{1}{2}$, 8)"/15 (16.5, 18, 19, 20.5) cm, ending with a WS row.

Shape Right Back Neck

Row 1 (RS): Ch3, work 6 (7, 7, 8, 8) dc pairs in patt, dc in next ch sp, turn.

Row 2 (WS): Work in patt to end.

Fasten off.

Shape Left Back Neck

With RS facing, rejoin yarn in 7th (8th, 8th, 9th, 9th) ch sp from end.

Row 1 (RS): Ch3, dc2tog over next 2 ch sps, continue in patt to end.

Row 2 (WS): Work in patt to end.

Fasten off.

Front

Work same as back until armhole shaping is complete. Armholes measure approximately 1$\frac{3}{4}$"/4.5 cm.

Shape Left Front Neck

Mark center ch-1 sp.

Row 1 (RS): Work in patt to center marker, ending with second leg of dc2tog in center ch sp, ch1, dc in center ch sp, turn.

Work 5 more rows even over these sts.

Next row (RS): Ch3, work 6 (7, 7, 8, 8) dc pairs in patt, dc in next ch sp, turn.

Continue in patt until same length as back to shoulder.

Fasten off.

Shape Right Front Neck

With RS facing, rejoin yarn in center ch-1 sp.

Row 1 (RS): Ch3, dc2tog over center ch sp and next ch sp, continue in patt to end.

Work 5 more rows even over these sts.

Next row (RS): Sl st in each dc2tog and ch sp until 6 (7, 7, 8, 8) dc pairs remain, ch3, dc2tog over next 2 ch sps, continue in patt to end.

Continue in patt until same length as back to shoulder.

Fasten off.

Finishing

Sew side seams. Sew shoulder seams.

Neck Edging

Join yarn at right front neck corner. Work 1 rnd sc around neck edge, sc in last st before end of rnd, ch4 for button loop, sc in same st as beginning of rnd.

Armhole Edging

Join yarn at side seam. Work 1 rnd sc around armhole edge. Fasten off.

Sew button to top left neck corner, opposite button loop.

Weave in ends. Block lightly.

Balboa

This tank has a twirly handkerchief hem and straps that cross in the back. The spatter dye on the linen-and-cotton blend yarn adds to the modern bohemian vibe.

SKILL LEVEL
Intermediate

SIZES
Women's Extra Small (Small, Medium, Large, Extra Large)

FINISHED MEASUREMENTS
Bust: $34^1/_4$ ($37^3/_4$, 41, $44^1/_2$, 48)"/87 (96, 104, 113, 122) cm

YARN
Fibra Natura Good Earth Adorn, medium weight #4 yarn (53% cotton, 47% linen; 204 yd./3.5 oz., 187 m/100 g per skein)
- 5 (6, 6, 7, 8) skeins #302 Adobe

HOOKS & NOTIONS
- US size H-8/5 mm crochet hook
- Tapestry needle

GAUGE
14 sts and 12 rows in hdc = 4"/10 cm

PATTERN NOTES
- See page 87 for a photo tutorial on hdc.
- This tank starts at the top of the bib and is worked down toward the hem.

Bib

Ch 34.

Row 1 (WS): Hdc in 3rd ch from hook and in each ch to end. 32 hdc.

Row 2 (RS): Ch2, turn, hdc in first hdc, sk 1, *hdc3 in next hdc, sk 2 hdc; rep from * to last 3 hdc, hdc3 in next hdc, sk 1 hdc, hdc2 in last hdc.

Row 3: Ch2, hdc in first hdc, hdc3 in each sp between groups of hdc to end, hdc in last hdc.

Row 4: Ch2, hdc3 in each sp between groups of hdc to end, hdc in last hdc.

Row 5: Ch2, hdc3 in each sp between groups of hdc to end, ending with hdc3 in 2nd ch of beginning ch-2.

Row 6: Ch2, hdc2 in first hdc, hdc3 in each sp between groups of hdc to end, ending with hdc2 in 2nd ch of beginning ch-2.

Row 7: Ch2, hdc2 in first hdc, hdc3 in each sp between groups of hdc to end, ending with hdc2 in 2nd ch of beginning ch-2.

Row 8: Ch2, hdc in first hdc, hdc3 in each sp between groups of hdc to end, ending with hdc in 2nd ch of beginning ch-2.

Row 9: Ch2, hdc3 in each sp between groups of hdc to end, ending with hdc in 2nd ch of beginning ch-2.

Row 10: Ch2, hdc3 in each sp between groups of hdc to end, ending with hdc in 2nd ch of beginning ch-2.

Row 11: Ch2, hdc2 in first hdc, hdc3 in each sp between groups of hdc to end, ending with hdc2 in 2nd ch of beginning ch-2.

Row 12: Ch2, hdc in first hdc, hdc3 in each sp between groups of hdc to end, ending with hdc2 in 2nd ch of beginning ch-2. 54 hdc. Do not turn at end of row.

Skirt

Ch 66 (78, 90, 102, 114), join with sl st to 2nd ch of beginning ch-2 of Row 12. 120 (132, 144, 156, 168) sts.

Rnd 1: Sl st to first sp between groups of hdc, ch2, hdc2 in same sp, hdc3 in each sp to end of bib, hdc3 in first ch, *sk 2 ch, hdc3 in next ch; rep from * until 2 ch rem, sk 2 ch, join with sl st to 2nd ch of beginning ch-2.

Rnds 2–12: Rep Rnd 1 eleven more times. Fasten off and break yarn.

Locate center back by folding the piece in half, matching the corners of the bib. Mark sp between groups of hdc at center back.

Rejoin yarn at marked sp.

Rnd 13: Ch2, hdc2 in same sp, hdc3 in next 2 (2, 3, 3, 4) sps between groups of hdc, [hdc2, ch1, hdc2] in next sp, hdc3 in next 5 (6, 6, 7, 7) sps between groups of hdc, [hdc2, ch1, hdc2] in next sp, hdc3 in next 5 (6, 6, 7, 7) sps between groups of hdc, [hdc2, ch1, hdc2] in next sp, hdcc3 in next 7 (7, 9, 9, 11) sps between groups of hdc, [hdc2, ch1, hdc2] in next sp, hdc3 in next 5 (6, 6, 7, 7) sps between groups of hdc, [hdc2, ch1, hdc2] in next sp, hdc3 in next 5 (6, 6, 7, 7) sps between groups of hdc, [hdc2, ch1, hdc2] in next sp, hdc3 in each sp between groups of hdc to end, join with sl st to 2nd ch of beginning ch-3.

Rnd 14: Ch2, hdc2 in same sp, *hdc3 in each sp between groups of hdc to ch-1 sp, [hdc2, ch1, hdc2] in ch-1 sp; rep from * 5 more times, hdc in each sp between groups of hdc to end, join with sl st to 2nd ch of beginning ch-3.

Rnds 15–30: Rep Rnd 14 sixteen more times.

Fasten off.

Finishing

Neck Edging

Work 1 rnd sc around upper edge of back and bib.

Straps

Ch 40. Join with sl st to upper corner of bib, ch1, sc in sl st and in each ch to end, sc3 in end of ch, working along other side of strap, sc in each ch to end.

Rep for second strap.

Mark attachment points for straps on back, 3"/7.5 cm on either side of center. Cross straps and sew in place, being careful not to twist straps.

Weave in ends. Block lightly.

Stitch Guide

Chain (ch)	Slip Stitch (sl st)

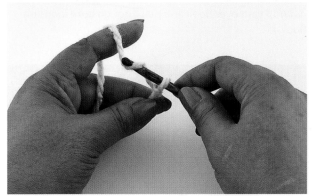

1. Begin with a slipknot on your hook. Loop yarn over the hook.

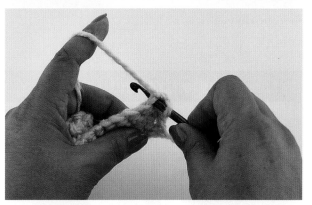

1. Insert hook into top of stitch.

2. Pull yarn through loop on hook. 1 chain made.

2. Loop yarn over hook.

3. Continue pulling the yarn through the loop on the hook until the required number of chains are made.

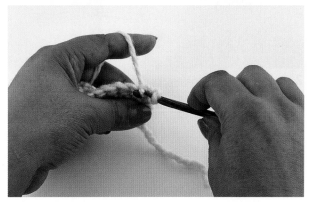

3. Pull yarn through stitch …

(continued)

4. . . . then through loop on hook.

Single Crochet (sc)

1. Insert hook into top of stitch.

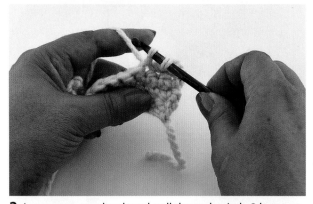

2. Loop yarn over hook and pull through stitch. 2 loops on hook.

3. Loop yarn over hook and pull through both loops on hook.

Single Crochet 2 Together (sc2tog)

1. Insert hook into top of stitch.

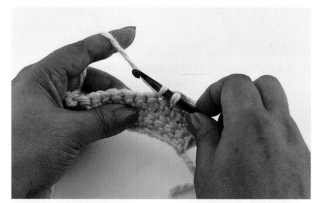

2. Loop yarn over hook and pull through stitch. 2 loops on hook.

3. Insert hook into top of next stitch.

4. Loop yarn over hook and pull through stitch. 3 loops on hook.

5. Loop yarn over hook and pull through all three loops on hook.

Half Double Crochet (hdc)

1. Loop yarn over hook.

2. Insert hook into top of stitch.

3. Loop yarn over hook and pull through stitch. 3 loops on hook.

(continued)

4. Loop yarn over hook and pull through all three loops on hook.

Half Double Crochet 2 Together (hdc2tog)

1. Loop yarn over hook.

2. Insert hook into top of stitch.

3. Loop yarn over hook and pull through stitch. 3 loops on hook.

4. Loop yarn over hook.

5. Insert hook into top of next stitch.

6. Loop yarn over hook and pull through stitch. 5 loops on hook.

7. Loop yarn over hook and pull through all five loops on hook.

Herringbone Half Double Crochet (hbhdc)

1. Loop yarn over hook.

2. Insert hook in stitch.

3. Loop yarn over hook and pull through stitch and first loop on hook. 2 loops on hook.

(continued)

4. Loop yarn over hook.

5. Pull through both loops on hook.

Double Crochet (dc)

1. Loop yarn over hook.

2. Insert hook in stitch.

3. Loop yarn over hook and pull through stitch. 3 loops on hook.

4. Loop yarn over hook.

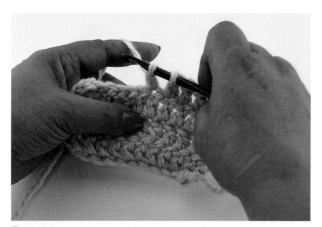

5. Pull through first two loops on hook.

6. Loop yarn over hook.

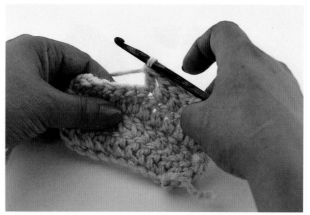

7. Pull through remaining two loops on hook.

Double Crochet 2 Together (dc2tog)

1. Loop yarn over hook.

2. Insert hook in stitch.

(continued)

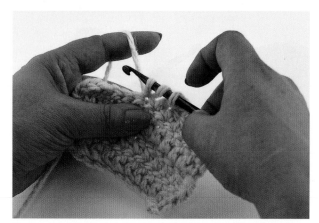

3. Loop yarn over hook and pull through stitch. 3 loops on hook.

4. Loop yarn over hook and pull through first two loops on hook.

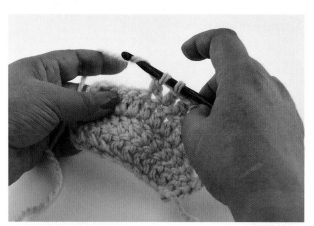

5. Loop yarn over hook.

6. Insert hook in next stitch.

7. Loop yarn over hook and pull through stitch. 4 loops on hook.

8. Loop yarn over hook.

9. Pull through first two loops on hook.

10. Loop yarn over hook.

11. Pull through remaining three loops on hook.

Single Crochet with Beads

1. String the appropriate number of beads onto the yarn before you begin.

2. Slide a bead up next to the hook.

3. Insert hook into stitch.

(continued)

4. Loop yarn over hook and pull through stitch, trapping the bead against the work.

5. Loop yarn over hook.

6. Pull through both loops on hook.

7. Beads appear on the side of the work facing away from you.

Yarn Resources

I am deeply grateful to the following companies for providing the beautiful yarn used for the projects in this book. While many of these yarns are readily available at your local yarn shop or craft store, you can also purchase directly from the companies at the websites shown below.

Berroco
www.berroco.com

Crystal Palace Yarns
www.straw.com

Fiesta Yarns
www.fiestayarns.com

Kollage Yarns
www.kollageyarns.com

LB Collection
www.lionbrand.com

Louet North America
www.louet.com

Patons and Bernat
www.yarnspirations.com

Premier Yarns and Deborah Norville Collection
www.premieryarns.com

Quince & Co.
www.quinceandco.com

Universal Yarn, Fibra Natura, and Nazli Gellin
www.universalyarn.com

Leading the Way in Crafts

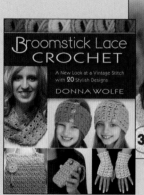

Discover inspiration and tips for your next project!